I061480e

What Stops You?

Overcome
Self-Sabotage
Personal and professional

Learn to Control your Thinking and Live the Life of your Dreams!

Darlene Braden, CHT

Copyright © 2006 Darlene Braden, db & company.
All rights reserved.
ISBN # 1-4196-2767-8

To order additional copies, please contact:
www.whatstopsyou.com

Table of Contents

Introduction:

Chapters:

Acknowledgments

I would like to thank my husband, Don, for giving me the best support possible during the course of writing this book. I would also like to thank my sons, Cassidy and Moshé, and my daughters, Summer, Jasmine, and Eden Rona. They are my life! My family has synergized with my thoughts at every dinner discussion, and they participated in my dreams for my clients throughout the years.

I would like to acknowledge my friend, John Breaux, owner of Vision Quest International. John helped me learn about business, presenting, training and helped me nourish my knowledge into a presentable forum.

I'd like to thank my parents, who supported me throughout my journey of education and experiences. Not only did they encourage me to earn my degree at the University of Utah, they also supported me with my nonaccredited, unquenchable desire to learn the Eastern metaphysical ways.

I acknowledge Anchor Point Institute for its brilliant leaders. The training was exquisite in its method, which taught me how to heal rather than just finding what was wrong. I thank all the trainers who facilitated me in my miraculous adventure of learning. I credit the founding fathers of NLP, John Grinder and Richard Bandler, who began investigating reasons that some therapists were able to effect powerful change and others were not. Their studies of Virginia Satir and Dr. Milton Erickson created the models we use today.

"The Pyramid Inside You" is based on the original model, "The Neurological Levels," originated by Robert Dilts. This is a brilliant model of the way we human beings process information at differing levels of neurology. I acknowledge Robert's efforts and appreciate the opportunity to synergize Robert's concepts. (For further information, visit the web site; www.nlpu.com.)

I deeply appreciate the instructors of the many certifications that I have participated in, throughout the years. What great people I have associated with in my years of learning!

Is This Book for You?

- Is something stopping you from achieving your goals?
- Do you know what is stopping you and why?
- Are you open-minded enough to discover more about yourself?
- Do you wonder why you just can't do something you have tried?
- Do you ever wonder why you do things that you attempt not to do?
- Are you aware that there is just something inside that stops you?
- Have you set the same goal over and over but have not quite achieved it for some mysterious reason?
- Are you ready to find out what stops you and take action to change it?

If so, this is the book you have been waiting for.

Do any of the following emotions seem to get in your way?

- Feelings of rejection
- Lack of control
- Powerlessness
- Intimidation
- Fear
- Anxiety
- Feeling unlovable

- Low self-esteem
- Loneliness

If these feelings often reoccur and if you have tried many ways to get rid of these feelings but they persist, and/or if you are on a path of self-discovery and feel stuck, this book is for you.

You will soon meet Anna, the character in this book whom you will learn to befriend, admire, and adore. Anna realizes that she needs all aspects of this book. Do you?

Suggestions to my readers:

To utilize this book fully, you have three options:

1. If you are not currently experiencing any particular problems, are open to learning, and would like a little direction in your life, feel free to **browse** through this book. It contains plenty of great ideas for you to contemplate.
2. If you are curious about new ways to think and experience the world and are open to changing limiting beliefs, **begin reading this book from cover to cover and fill out some of the exercises.** You will learn many ways of looking at situations differently, and you will begin to take positive action on these matters at a conscious or unconscious level.
3. If you seem to be severely stuck in life, I recommend reading this book **slowly, word for word.** I recommend **reading it twice and going through each exercise with much thought.** The second

time, review the material, underline key phrases, write your thoughts in the margins, do the exercises, and commit to changing your life. You will then experience positive change, start to rewire old thought patterns, and begin to heal. You may also want to **work with a life coach or therapist** to assist you in your processes of change.

If you choose to simply browse the book or read the chapters out of order, I invite you to make sure you look at Chapter Fourteen, "Evaluating Your Performance," to bookend your learnings.

No matter how you choose to utilize this book, I hope that the concern and love I feel for you will assist you in achieving greater love for yourself – a love that I know, without a doubt, you deserve. I hope to assist you in believing in yourself. You are not alone, and I support you in your journey.

My Intent

O ne of my very important intents is to help you make more money! When you overcome your internal limitations, you will be able to set more appropriate goals and follow through to the success you desire. This book focuses on personal **and** business self-sabotage. It is important to note that professional self-sabotage **is really** personal sabotage, yet in a business environment. For example, fear of success, fear of failure, and limiting beliefs about money – like thinking you don't deserve money or that rich people are lucky – are really personal issues, aren't they? So as you discover your possible business limitations, my intent is for you to understand that **you and your thinking patterns** are the key to your business success.

Another of my intents is to give you the gift of my knowledge, experience, time, and love. I certainly don't know everything, yet what I do know, I offer. I believe in you and your ability to affect many other people in a positive way. I present all I have for your benefit and the benefit of all of those you touch. This book will help you discover, decipher, sort, and integrate conflicts with the result of alignment and peace.

I run about 15 to 20 miles a week, and with each run I come back with another chapter completed. I think about my audience constantly; I visualize you while I run and contemplate what you might need and how to say it. (If you are ever going to write a book, I suggest that you take up running.) I would like you to get to know me as a friend, support, and guide. I have walked the earth for decades now, searching for methods and ways to assist those in need. Thank you for letting me share with you.

Remember that life is a journey, not a destination. If you have heard or read my words, I am honored, and I ask God to assist you in your life. You and I are now beginning our relationship from a distance, and I pray that you find the peace you are searching for.

Now it's time for you to take action, dig in, and take this self-help book at your own pace. Are you ready? Let's get going.

Preface

The reason I wrote this book is to assist you in finding peace and meaning in your life and to *live the life of your dreams*. In order to accomplish this, I use a variety of techniques to guide you, from Eastern healing arts and philosophy to modern tangible techniques. Some of these tools include Neuro Linguistic Programming (NLP) strategies, energy balancing, hypnotherapy concepts, unconscious communication, affirmations, and behaviors such as actions and skill sets.

This book will help you understand **how** you process your thinking patterns, so that you can control your thoughts. To begin understanding your thinking processes, **you must first understand the workings of the unconscious mind.** The unconscious mind can think of millions if not billions of pieces of information at the same time – unlike the conscious mind, which can process only about five to nine pieces of information at the same moment. For example, while driving a car, your mind is automatically processing at least 20 to 30 pieces of information at the same time. Can you imagine what these pieces are?

How many things is your unconscious aware of right now? Stop and notice what you see, hear, and feel. Were you aware of your computer humming, cars passing on the street, a clock ticking, or the rhythm of your breathing? Before I asked the question, you probably were not aware of these pieces of information on a conscious level, yet on an unconscious level you may have been.

Your unconscious typically uses a large percentage of your mind, and conscious thought is only a tiny portion. I have heard it said that we use 1 one-hundredth of a percent of our total brain capacity. It has been said that Einstein used only 3 percent of his abilities. I imagine that no one really knows the exact percentage, so let's say that the average individual accesses only about 2 percent or so of his or her brain during life, and this 2 percent represents the logical part of the mind. Public schools, for the most part, are structured to access, teach, and train the logical, left-brained side of your mind. The other 98 percent of the brain is the unconscious, which involves intuition, sensing, creativity, and spirituality, and it is more metaphorical. Most people do not know how to use this 98 percent.

So what is the unconscious mind? Simply put, the unconscious is that of which you are not consciously aware – the place where all learning and change happens.

One of the most common methods I use throughout this book is NLP. NLP explores in very precise terms the images, sounds, and feelings that make up our inner and outer world. How do you know that a pleasant memory is pleasant? Or how do you know if you are happy or scared? How do you code your experiences in your mind in terms of pictures, sounds, and body sensations? By internally shifting how you see, hear, and feel, you can shift your experience. By using NLP techniques, you can discover the answers to your questions.

For example, picture yourself basking in the warmth of the noonday sun. As you feel the wind glide across your skin, close your eyes and let all the cares of your world simply blow away. Feel the temperature of your skin. (Pause and take a breath.) Notice what sounds you hear, if anything. Sense the emotions that you feel, now, as the pressures of life are lifted away with your thoughts. (Pause and take another deep breath.) Notice what it is like to be here on this beach.

OK, let that go, and in contrast, let's shift your thoughts. Imagine one of your loved ones in your home, and as you enter the living room, you discover someone in the dark shadows holding a gun to your loved one's head. You are overtaken by the panic you notice in your loved one's eyes. You can see a metal weapon pressed against his or her temple and tears pouring down his or her cheeks. You can see everything in slow motion as you try to calm the situation at hand, but you are too far away to help. You can hear every breath from your loved one and the heaviness of the fear that spreads throughout the air. A deep feeling of helplessness begins to overtake you.

Now pause and let that all go. Please take a breath and return to the present moment. Which of the two situations was clearer and more vivid? Which was more open to your peripheral vision? What sounds did you hear with each example? Were the sounds soft and flowing, or were they piercing, sharp, or muffled? Did you feel your heart rate and blood pressure change by a mere thought? And to think that the two scenarios were not even real, yet you felt a dramatic physiological shift.

How profound is that? By a mere thought you were able to change your bodily functions on a conscious and an unconscious level. Many changes occurred in your body, including hormone production. If a thought can produce such dramatic change, then isn't it important that you learn to control your thoughts? Isn't it exciting to know that you can control and create your dreams for the future?

Our thoughts are powerful.

Whether you are a full-time **stay-at-home dad/mom, homemaker, network marketing distributor, loan officer, realtor,** or other occupation, it will be exciting for you to follow a simple or difficult issue through this book as you learn how to recognize and control your thoughts.

You may want to lose weight forever. You may want to work on relationship issues, learn to be punctual, or understand fear of success or failure. What do you want?

WHAT STOPS YOU?

Chapter One:

ANNA'S TRAVELS
Deciding to Start

W ith my unquenchable desire to enjoy the fresh mountain air and to keep my body fat well below the normal range for a woman, I started out on my daily run. As I crossed the street to my well-known trail along the frontage road of the beautiful Rocky Mountain foothills, I was aware of my good fortune. As I approached my second mile, the trance state that keeps my addiction going enveloped me, and I began to contemplate that day's lunch date with Anna.

Anna was an old friend from high school, which I might add was years ago. She looked me up and called me out of the blue. She had heard that I was a business and personal life coach, and she was desperate for help. After high school she moved back East, and I hadn't heard from her for years. On the phone she sounded sad and drenched with pain. Her voice was weak and hollow. When we finally ended our conversation, I found my thoughts reaching back in time.

I remembered how we used to dream of our futures. We just knew we would be rich and successful. We vividly imagined our ultimate ranch in Texas, breeding horses. We dreamed that we would own international companies. We fantasized about what our handsome husbands would be like, as the two of us enjoyed the happiness we deserved.

"Anna. Oh, Anna Marie, what has happened?" I asked myself in contemplative thought, as the pavement passed below my feet. In my mind I heard the echo of her sad voice on the phone that gave messages of depression, hopelessness, and pain. I continued on, in reflection.

After over an hour of running, which seemed like 10 minutes, I reached my destination: an ice-cold drink of water and a warm shower. My muscles were fatigued, and while the water rushed over my head, I realized that my hamstrings were especially tight on that crisp fall morning. It must have been because of the fight with gravity on the steep hills that sweep the area. My stiffness could also be attributed to the speed at which I ran in my deep state of concentration.

I stretched a bit in the limited space available and breathed in a large quantity of misty air. I focused my thoughts toward the principles of gravity as the steam filled the room. Obeying natural law makes life much easier. Rolling downhill is more effortless than climbing, yet there is some reason that I like to run the hills. I decided that after an immense upward exertion, it is nice to be rewarded with the opportunity to recover a bit and glide smoothly towards a lower elevation.

I wondered why most people have an innate need to strive, climb, reach for the top, and progress.

Considering all the mountains, hills, and valleys in life, I reviewed the age-old questions: "Why is it so hard for people to find peace? Why is it so hard for people to find the correct way to push and appropriately progress?"

I reflected back to Anna and wondered, "Why is Anna so tormented? What road has she been on, and what makes her path so difficult? Why doesn't she ever seem to get a downhill break in life?"

After drying off and feeling comfortable in my fuzzy slippers, I made myself some hot chocolate and clicked on a morning television show. I watched all sorts of local news and cooking tips and heard interviews with new authors and actresses. The national news is always the most turbulent and eye catching. I found myself glued to the set as I heard about the latest excitement in the Middle East and the nation's weather with hurricanes and Mother Nature's many other dramas. Again I asked myself, "Why do some people find peace in the midst of turmoil and others do not?"

In the years that I have sat, one-on-one, face-to-face with clients, I have discovered many possible answers to these questions. I have observed many similarities in my client's issues and desires. Each guest in my office comes with seemingly unique pressures and pain. Interestingly enough, many times the previous client was experiencing similar problems. Each and every client wants freedom, choice, power, safety, acceptance, and peace. If I asked a congregation of one thousand people how many of them wanted peace, freedom, and safety, I wonder how many hands would go up in the air. Based on this information, I felt that I might have some ideas to assist Anna, and I decided that I would set my intent for this lunch with my long-time friend: to be a listening ear and possibly her guide.

Each and every client wants freedom, choice, power, safety, acceptance, and peace.

Quite frankly, when I have lunch with friends, I sometimes like to turn off my listening ear, and occasionally I like lunch to be psychobabble free. I like to just talk about things I can see and feel, yet somehow that day I felt an incredibly deep desire to be a girlfriend and give Anna assistance if at all possible.

I tossed on a white sweater with black slacks and my first pair of covered-toe shoes since the temperature had cooled. After exerting this morning, I decided that being cold was out of the question, so I grabbed a light jacket in case of a chilly episode.

When I reached the restaurant, I looked for my old friend, the bubbly, zealous, and beautiful Anna-Banana, as we used to lovingly tease her. I remembered her silky-dark hair and small frame. I could replay in my mind her youthful, light-green eyes that were crystal clear like a fresh mountain lake.

Finally, I felt a hand on my shoulder. "Darlene?" someone said gently. I slowly turned to see a wind-torn, middle-aged woman with deep pain apparent in her eyes. Her well-fed frame was a bit slumped, and her dull, lifeless hair was randomly tousled. Nonetheless, I naturally and immediately felt the connection with Anna that I had experienced years ago and gave her a big smile. I offered her a warm hug and expressed that I was so glad to meet up with her again.

We were seated in a private booth overlooking a beautiful mountain river. We started with small talk and eventually began to catch up on the last few decades. She stated that she had been a failure in business and personal relationships. She was financially upside down, out of work, and ready to lose the lease she had on an old apartment. She had two children out of wedlock when she was a teen, and she struggled terribly while raising them alone. Her kids hadn't spoken to her in years and had managed to move on with their lives without her. She was currently in a tumultuous relationship with many fears about her pattern of choosing men who abused her physically and emotionally. Her only joy was her two Golden Retrievers, King and Tahoe, whom she loved and adored.

I, in turn, explained my journey of being married at 19, having five great kids, and going through the trials of divorce after 21 years of marriage. During this period I experienced the death of my brother from cancer and my best friend's death from a car crash. With emotion, I relayed how my back was broken in this accident, which necessitated 10 years of acupuncture, spinal touch, and meditation.

All this pain and all my questions led me to my higher education in human development, psychology, drug treatment, and studies of hypnosis, NLP, and the unconscious mind. I told her some of the things I had learned and how I finally put it all together. I exclaimed that I was now married to a new husband who was supportive and awesome. (Yes, there is peace after all!)

Yes, there can be peace after all!

It never seems to fail that upon hearing the words "hypnosis and the unconscious mind," others are inquisitive. As Anna inquired, I began to explain to her that about 98 percent of the brain is operated by the unconscious. When we understand how the unconscious works, we can begin to have power and control in our lives.

Anna said that she could feel the contentment I portrayed. She could sense that I had a congruent manner and was "in the moment" with her. She wondered what I did to find peace within myself in this crazy world.

"I know you are a successful life coach, and if there is anything you can teach me, I would be grateful," she said.

"Anna," I said, "Peace is not a thing. It is not an object or a destination. Peace is a state of mind." I explained to her what I had learned about peace.

I have spent years analyzing what peace is, how to be aware of it, and how to achieve it. Let me share with you the definition of peace that I have come up with. Peace is when there is a void of conflict. Peace is the state of being in one piece and not in conflict.

Peace = One Piece

"Anna, you have been sabotaging yourself," I said. "You have been acting out of one side or the other side of your mind your whole life. You have never been in one piece, have you? Either you please part of your mind and the other part is mad, or you please the other side of your mind and the other side is mad. It feels very confusing, and you certainly don't need a spouse to mess it all up and cause more conflict. You have enough contention and conflict just inside your own skin. Am I right?"

"Oh yes," she said. "I seem to be experiencing constant torture. I change boyfriends, I change jobs, I drink too much, and I have contemplated taking my life much too often. I can't seem to put things together. As soon as I start to become successful, something happens. Something stops me, and I don't know what it is. I am so frustrated, and I get so mad at myself. I can say that I truly hate myself."

"My friend, I imagine that every day you can't be rid of yourself. Every day you eat with yourself, sleep with yourself, and even go to the bathroom with yourself. Am I right?" I asked.

She gave a slight smile while flipping one of her earrings around and around.

"So," I said, "it is pretty important to love yourself if you can't be rid of 'you,' isn't it? Do you agree?"

"How?" she asked. "How? Just tell me how."

Let's define conflict and sabotage, so that we can make sure we are both talking about the same thing.

CONFLICT: A struggle; clashing of views or statements; to meet in opposition; to be antagonistic.

SABOTAGE: An act or process tending to hamper or hurt or deliberate subversion; destructive or obstructive action carried on by a civilian or enemy agent to hinder a nation's war effort. *Webster's New Edition

According to these definitions, if we are at war with our own business or self-interest, we are committing sabotage. In other words, we are at **war with ourselves,** not with someone else. The word "sabotage" does not apply if I reach over the table and knock your fork on the floor. This would not be sabotage; it would just be mean or weird. Yet, if you and I were on the same team having a spaghetti-eating contest and I knocked your fork off the table, this would be sabotage because I would be hurting myself or my own team.

It is common to have opposing parts and conflicts.

We might think of our bodies as a whole company. If my head wars against my heart, this would be a form of sabotage, would it not? If part of me wants something different than another part does, it feels awful. Part of me wants to eat and gorge, and part of me wants to be thin. We have all heard of "the fat man versus the thin man" conflict – the two opposing parts that never agree about food and fitness. One part wants to eat and be comfortable and feels entitled to enjoy life, and the other part wants to be thin and sexy for many reasonable as well as absurd reasons. As the saying goes, "The twain never shall meet." Most of us have these two opposing parts. For example, part of me did not want to go running this morning. Trust me:

part of me screamed, "No! Sleep in." Yet the other part that has a goal to train for a race was just stronger today. Have you ever felt this way?

Now we don't all have multiple personality disorder, yet we **all** have parts of our minds that make us feel moody or different on various days.

"OK," Anna said, "last week I was ready to check myself into the funny farm. I had really given up, and I wondered if I would start to wander the streets and talk to myself!"

The goal is to have all our emotional and mental parts in agreement; then sabotage does not exist. If all of me wants something, and if I know how to do it and I believe I can, there is nothing to stop me. Right? I then experience peace and can enjoy the present moment. I have the tools to **go forward towards my dreams and live the life I want,** with power, choice and control.

Anna said, "If only I could have a therapist/coach to assist me. I have never known where to turn and what direction to take. I have been to numerous therapists and counselors and seem to return to the same old patterns I've always had. Is there any way that you could help me?"

I thought for a moment and then slowly and methodically told her what my dad used to say. He said, **"If you don't love your passion enough to charge top dollar for it, you don't believe in it enough."** He also added, **"If you don't believe in your passion enough to give it away, you don't be-lieve in it enough."**

Anna quickly pulled out a note pad and paper. She

said, "I better start taking notes. This is getting good!"

I explained my policy based on my dad's advice. "I charge top dollar for my sessions. Clients expect to pay a hefty price for peace, and they report that no amount of money is too much for mental and physical health." I told her that I also have a policy of offering my services at no charge when I feel right about it. When the particular person I am working with is complete and whole, I offer that slot for my next guest.

Anna nearly jumped out of her skin. Her eyes glared straight through me.

"I would be pleased and honored to consider you, Anna, as my next opportunity to coach, love, and offer my time," I said.

I then explained, "Anna, I would absolutely love to work with you on the following conditions. Are you ready to hear them?"

She leaned over the table between us. Her lime-colored eyes glistened and her countenance softened. She looked so beautiful at that moment. She told me that she was more open than ever before and that she would climb the highest mountain to get results. Anna grabbed my hands and looked me in the eye. "What can I do?" she said.

I told her my rules when working with someone at no cost. "If you will adhere to my rules," I told Anna, "then in return I will give you my heart, soul, expertise, time, and energy."

My rules are:

1. Be open to learning and be willing to change.
2. Never miss an appointment. Give two days' notice, please, if you need to change the time, and remember that no-shows are billed at my premium rate.
3. Be willing to complete all assignments and tasks each week.
4. Read other books and pamphlets that I recommend to enhance and complement what I have taught you.
5. Teach what you have learned to someone else during the process. Deep and lasting change occurs when you teach concepts and principles to someone else.

With an animated response, Anna said, "When do we get started?"

I told Anna that when I returned to my office, I would e-mail her a copy of **My Beliefs and Principles for Change**. I told her that she needed to read them **before our first meeting** because they would help her understand my beliefs that support all my teachings.

I asked her to start writing down her dreams for the future and to start focusing on all the things she wants out of life.

Anna said, "What in the heck is a dream? I haven't been able to dream forever. I've been to busy fighting for my life!"

I said, "I remember in high school we used to dream of having a ranch in Texas. Do you remember that? Also when you were a child, didn't you ever

12

press your nose against the window and gaze out into the distance imagining all the things you wanted to do and be, in the future, in vivid color?

"A dream is a future picture and feeling, created in a state of relaxation and freedom. A dream is what you want as an end result, without any hesitation of how to achieve it. Our dreams cause us to live with **purpose, determination and passion**. When one gives up their dreams they emotionally die. Have you ever seen the walking dead; people with no purpose or passion?

"So Anna, begin to create your dreams; make them big and full of energy. In the weeks to come, I will show you how to make appropriate changes to fully live the life of your dreams!

Anna looked like she was in the starting blocks. She was ready to start her life again.

Then I said, "Let's spend a little more time over lunch to get you going. Besides, the cheesecake is so very good." We both chuckled.

Chapter Two:

WHAT'S IN YOUR BACKPACK?

Preparing for Change

*D*ear Anna,

    I really enjoyed having lunch with you the other day. Reconnecting sure brings back a lot of memories of our past. I am looking forward to our new journey together.

    Here is the document that I said I would send you before our first coaching session, which discusses my core beliefs and principles for change. Please print it out and in a quiet moment read through the pages and ponder and digest all that applies to you. I want you to wonder, uncover, and contemplate what your own core beliefs are.

Darlene Braden's Beliefs

My core beliefs have come from my life's experiences, both positive and negative. The culmination of what I've learned in life, to this point, has formed my beliefs and my choices. This book is written with my core beliefs in mind.

I believe in God.

I believe in God. You may refer to God as the Everywhere Spirit, Heavenly Father, Higher Power, Allah, or whatever name works within your beliefs. I want you as my reader to know that I refer to God often, whether spoken, written, or silently etched in my mind. I also believe in Jesus as a perfect example of love, forgiveness, strength, wisdom, goal setting, focus, identity, and perfect faith in life's process. I believe that recognition of something greater than yourself, is important to healing and discovery.

I believe in modeling successful people.

Modeling is an excellent way for us to learn as we look at self-actualized individuals. In my practice I refer often to revered leaders such as Gandhi, Mother Teresa, and the Dalai Lama. I have been known to use Superman and Spiderman (my favorite) as models or heroes because of their integrity, consistency, and humility. How about modeling Bugs Bunny's attitude and focus? I imagine that Bugs Bunny has tremendous self-esteem and an unwaveringly positive attitude.

I believe that all men
and women have common desires.

All men and women have common, universal desires, which are freedom, safety, peace, acceptance, and the feeling that they are not alone. All men and women want to be free to be themselves, or, to put it another way, **TO BE**. All people strive to achieve these desires in various ways. We have fought world wars and civil wars for freedom. We strive for both physical and emotional safety. We search for acceptance from our parents and those around us. I believe that all men and women have an unconscious need to please their parents regardless of their parents' involvement or actions. I believe that even terrorists or criminals unconsciously want to please their parents. The family of origin (parents and siblings) is a great place to begin healing. This book does not necessarily address the family of origin, yet I recommend healing the family dynamics as an important part of pro-gression. If you want further information on healing family dynamics, I highly recommend the book *Love's Hidden Symmetry* by Bert Hellinger.

I know that this book is just a guide or recipe, if you will, to help you extract and **put together all that you already have inside you.** Possibly your resources have been buried alive or hidden. Possibly life has just "slimed you." Nonetheless, you are about to uncover your resources.

I believe wise men and women, seek wise counsel.

I don't and can't know everything. I surely don't know how to fix my car and I certainly don't know how to milk a cow. At one point in time, I didn't know how to use some computer programs, such as budgeting or word processing software.

To overcome this lack of knowledge, I sought advice and assistance from experts in these areas. Today, unlike other times in history, we depend more upon others to exist in this world. In centuries past, a single family was more able to sustain basic life needs through agricultural independence. In this day and age, we need to reach out to others' expertise more than ever and call "Uncle" when we need help.

It does not matter what occurred in your life; you can still heal **with the appropriate resources and knowledge.** I have worked with incarcerated delinquents, rape victims, and even murderers in secure facilities. I have seen these people develop wholeness from gentle guidance and specific treatments and resources.

As we seek wise counsel, it is important to learn appropriate skills. We have all heard it said, "If you know what to do, then you will figure out the how."

I operate under the opposite paradigm. I believe: **If we know what to do, we don't necessarily know how to do it.**

I have seen too many people who absolutely know **what** they ought to do yet search desperately for **how** to achieve the task. In most churches we hear, "Be nice, be good, be kind, repent, and love your enemy." We go about trying to do all these nice things, and then one day we bellow, **"How** do I love my enemy? **How** do I forgive my abusive father? **How** do I give up alcohol?"

I imagine you already know **what** you are supposed to do, like being nice, being good, and forgiving others. Yet, your big question is, "How?" Am I right? Well, you are in luck. This book addresses **how:** how to forgive, how to overcome fear, how to love yourself, and much more.

I believe in karma:
"What goes around comes around."

I believe in karma. What we give out will come back to us, yet not necessarily in this mortal life. I believe that this mortal life is part of the greater whole and that we continually progress even beyond death. I have heard of an ancient belief that a butterfly in eastern Asia may have some indirect effect on the typhoons in Hawaii because we are all part of a bigger picture. According to one of the funeral homes in my area, 200 to 250 people attend the average funeral. Each life directly or indirectly affects many people.

For example, say that you express anger at your mail carrier. The mail carrier goes home and is rude to his spouse, who is then short with their child. The child is then pushy with his friend. The friend is then rude to her school teacher. The upset teacher calls her sister in Chicago and ruins her day. The woman's husband has just about had it with his moody wife, so he goes to the bar. He ends up deciding to go to an old girlfriend's apartment and gets hit by a truck....

Oh my gosh, this cycle could continue forever, and the anger you showed towards your mail carrier weeks or months ago may come back to you in a negative way some day. As the saying goes, "What goes around comes around." So when your teen says to you, "Leave me alone! It's my life!" at an opportune time, you may teach him or her, "No, it isn't!"

I believe that to find inner peace, one cannot heal the mind without healing the body *and* spirit.

Most of society today acknowledges that mending the mind along with the body is important. For example, we energy workers utilize a network of referrals with the recognition that no one modality is all that is needed. On occasion, I refer my clients who are emotionally stuck to a massage therapist to unlock body memory. When the client returns to me, he or she is ready to move forward. A massage therapist may send a client to me to address emotional issues when the body may not be responding due to these emotions. Traumatic events are coded in your neurology and physiology, and to heal these events, the body sensations and feelings must be acknowledged so that the client can shift the emotions appropriately.

In my experience, individuals stagnate when they do not acknowledge their spiritual growth for purposes beyond **just themselves.** They seem to hit a wall in the healing process until they acknowledge others as important factors in their lives. One way I encourage individuals to achieve this is to give them seven pennies – one for each day of the week – on which to make a daily wish. But, the criterion is to make a wish for **someone else** each day. In most cases, the client comes back at a new level of evolution ready to learn in a whole new way.

I believe that when you LOVE and HONOR yourself, your life works!

Deep and honest self-love and honor naturally cause one to take appropriate actions, have appropriate boundaries, and make opportune choices that are clear of emotion. Something wonderful happens when we achieve actualized love and honor of ourselves. Since we are always with ourselves, everywhere we go, this self-love is vitally important. Self-honor causes greater physical and financial health and spiritual growth. All things seem to fall into place, and perceptions of situations become accurate rather than too large to handle. When one has self-love, life seems to have a larger perspective. It is like being above the maze of life rather than hiding deep inside with a limited perspective. Something magical happens when you truly find out who you are and you honestly love and sincerely honor yourself.

I believe that we create our own experiences; what we focus on we give power to.

If we focus on anger, anger will have power. If we focus on love, love has power. If we focus on a dream of how we want things to be, we will live our dreams, when using the right tools.

How we choose to think about our lives, others and experiences, will have power to project us in to the reality we create.

I believe that when we learn our lesson, our trial goes away.

I believe that somehow, on a deep, unconscious level, we invite or leave an opening for certain trials to be part of our life. I believe that life is our teacher, and problems exist because we need to learn something. Have you ever watched a friend with a particular trial or problem and realized that if you had that problem, you would be able to solve it, or you would never have had that problem in the first place? When we gather and assimilate learnings about our circumstances, then the problem is no longer necessary. When we learn what we need to learn, the problem goes away.

Presuppositions About My Clients

I believe the following statements about each client who comes into my office:

1. Each person's perception is his or her reality.

2. **People always do the best they can with what they know.**
3. **All actions, thoughts, and feelings have a positive intent.**
4. **More choice is better than no choice.**
5. **What you focus on, you give power to.**
6. **People are born good, all with different gifts.**
7. **Most people have all the ingredients they need; they just need help with the recipe.**

Darlene Braden's Principles for Change

As we begin, it is important to recognize that all parts of your mind are involved as you read this book. You are reading with your:

- **Logical head.**
- **Passionate heart.**
- **Physical body sensations.**
- **Gut feelings.**
- **Spirit or soul.**

Your logical **mind** does not always agree with the passion of your passionate **heart.** Possibly your **gut** feeling does not always agree with what your **body** wants. Does your **spirit** always agree with what your **heart** and **body** desire?

Please understand that your unconscious is alive and well. To elaborate this point, let me ask you this question: **Did you roll off your bed last night?** Most likely, you did not. Why? Because your unconscious mind was awake and knew where the side of the bed was. This proves we have so much power within us that we are not utilizing to the fullest!

Limiting beliefs imprint at a young age.

Based on what I have learned in my training and years of experience working with clients, most limiting beliefs and actions stem from past events that occur at age 18 or earlier. Traumatic events may create limiting beliefs that imprint in your mind and body and retard or stop your development at the age the trauma occurred. You may halt progressing in certain aspects, which causes you to remain developmentally stuck at that particular age. As you biologically age, part of your mind does not progress in this specific area in regards to the trauma, and it metaphorically manifests as an unhealed child within you. Part of your mind matures and copes in an adult manner. The inner child that is retarded or stopped in its progression may show up as feelings such as lack of control, not feeling safe, lack of power, and so on. At times it is very important to acknowledge and heal the past.

Progress fits into three categories.

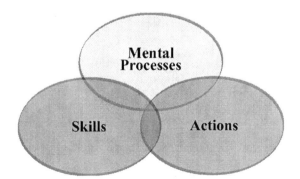

- **Actions:** Take action! Do it, or stop doing it!
- **Skills**: How well do you do things?
- **Mental processes**: Beliefs, perceptions, emotions, and ways of looking at things are the basis for all actions and skills.

Actions, skills, and mental processes are the three important aspects in every intervention for desired change. They are all equally important. Working on one at a time is recommended, yet I believe that to change we must acknowledge **all** three areas. In each chapter we will look closely at the **actions, skills, and/or mental processes** that are **stopping you from success.**

These are my truths and my realities. If they work for you, then please read on. The premises by which I operate are layered upon these foundations. What are your beliefs?

This is an interactive book. To help you discover more about yourself, fill in all the spaces provided, and grab a notebook to record your thoughts as we proceed.

Chapter Three:

ANNA'S NEW MAP
The Balanced Living Wheel

" **G**ood morning, Anna. How are you today?" I asked as she entered my office.

She replied, "Well, as I was sitting in your waiting room, I realized that I didn't sleep a wink last night. I am exhausted and preoccupied because I am meeting with the bankruptcy attorney at noon. I got a call from my boyfriend last night, and he said that he needed time to think about our relationship. He admitted that he wasn't that attracted to me anymore. Anyway, I am here in body but I am having a hard time focusing. Sorry."

I realized that one of Anna's patterns was to play the victim. I let that go for now, because soon she would understand the power of her thoughts and would be able to learn tools to diagnose such limited thinking patterns. She then would be able to shift her thoughts into resourceful actions.

"Let's continue our discussion that we started over lunch. I am pleased to be your coach, Anna, and I appreciate your willingness to learn," I responded.

"Were you able to read **My Beliefs and Principles for Change?**" I asked.

"Oh yes," she replied. "I sat up late into the night with my electric blanket and dogs by my side. As I read, I could feel your words of wisdom. I took some time to contemplate your basic beliefs, and I really want to open myself up to look at what I believe. I realized that I have never really sat down and thought about my general beliefs. I am so ready to look at all this stuff. Also, I understand your principles for change, and I really like that you address change in the three areas of actions, skills, and mental processes. All other coaches and therapists I have been to only focus on actions and behaviors. I am excited that you will show me how to do things instead of just telling me what to do."

"Last week when we had lunch, we defined peace, conflict, and sabotage. Let's review a few examples in each area," I said.

In my opinion, the only way to sabotage yourself is to have conflict: **Part of you** wants this and **part** wants that. Does that seem familiar?

Here are some examples of **professional and personal sabotage** that you may be experiencing:

Personal sabotage may occur in relationships, childhood issues, self-esteem, and identity issues. You may be "trying" to pursue a task or goal, and you feel that something deep inside is stopping you from success in these areas.

Professional sabotage may interfere with the ability to sell, prospect, make calls, and accomplish tasks. Professional sabotage may include beliefs about your chosen profession, money, or yourself. You feel as though there is just something stopping you, possibly right before you reach success.

We will be using the **same models** to help you discover what stops you in both the **professional and personal** realms. If you think about it, if you are sabotaging yourself in your professional life, **it is really personal sabotage that is occurring.** For example, if you are not asking for referrals frequently, it may be that you are afraid of rejection or are not "sold" enough on the benefits of your product. In each case, these are **personal aspects regarding business** that need to be redefined and implemented with new ways of thinking.

Let's get to work. Are you ready? Are all of your parts ready? If not, let's talk to the part that is ready.

Setting goals is really important. There are plenty of rah-rah seminars that get you pumped up to set goals. They say, "Picture the goal; go for it. Do what it takes, and whatever it takes is whatever it takes."

Now in part I agree. Goal setting through visual pictures is important, but rah-rah is only a surface motivator. If you are going to make deep and lasting change you must take a vital step **before** setting goals.

This step is to know where you are now, in your present state, before the journey. For example, let's pretend that you are in a new profession and you are now a road assistance operator. Your job is to answer the phones and help the other person on the other end of the line. Let's say you answered the phone and heard someone with a strong Spanish accent say, "Hello, I wondered if you could tell me the way to Disneyland. I want to take my family, and I need to know how to get there." Would you be able to assist that person with directions?

What if the phone rang again and you heard someone with a heavy English accent say, "Hello there, I was wondering if you could give me the directions to Disneyland." Could you assist this person as well? My guess is that you would need to gather some information from your callers before you could answer concisely. What information would you need? What questions would you ask them? Would you ask them their Social Security numbers? Would you ask them their measurements?

Anna gave a bit of a smirk, which was fun for me to see.

No, you would simply need to ask them **where they are coming from or where they are now.** The directions from Mexico to California are very different than the directions from England to California.

"With this in mind," I said, "before we begin, Anna, let's find out specifically where you are now in life in the 10 life categories shown in the Balanced Living Wheel Self-Assessment."

Please use Anna's filled-in graph as a guide to fill out your own graph.

Balanced Living Wheel
Self-Assessment

Name: *Anna*
My Professional Goal: <u>Make comfortable sales</u>
My Personal Goal: <u>Lose 25 pounds</u>

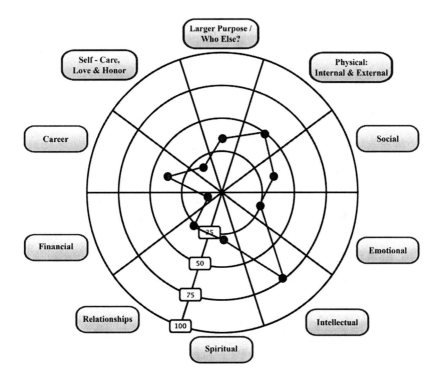

Anna's Assessment Before Her Journey

As you look at the graph, you will see that the center of the circle is 0 and the outer edge represents 100.

Zero = the worst you could be.
100 = the best you can be.

Please rate yourself in each category. Where are you now in your life? This assessment is meant to be current, so think of where you are **today**, not where you want to be or where you have been. Remember to separate the categories in your mind as much as possible, realizing that this can be a challenge because all the categories affect each other's ratings. If you were to ignore and delete all the other categories, focusing on one at a time, what would you rate yourself in each single area?

Remember, it is possible to be 100 because it is not the world's 100; it is your 100. Let's say you are a body builder and you just won the Mr. or Ms. Olympia title. Well, you would certainly be at 100, yes? OK, then, what would you do the next day? You would go back to the gym, wouldn't you? It takes effort to maintain 100, so being 100 would be where a person would rate himself or herself at the moment, and this 100 would need to be maintained in the future.

Anna said cynically, "Ya, right. I don't think I need to worry about being 100 in that category. I just wondered what you would do if you needed a negative number because the graph doesn't seem to go that low. I think I am really just 0 in all the areas."

We went through each category, one by one. She found that, although she rated herself very low, she could clearly see the areas that needed improvement.

I continued to explain to her that the most important question was yet to come. Now, after you have put a dot in the middle of each category, ask yourself: What stops me from being 100? Whatever stops you is where you want to focus your efforts.

When it is your turn to fill out your wheel, you may:
1. Use the wheel in the book.
2. Draw a wheel on a sheet of paper.
3. Go to my web site and **download a FREE copy of the wheel. www.whatstopsyou.com**

Balanced Living Wheel
Self-Assessment

Name: _____ Date: _____
My Professional Goal: _____
My Personal Goal: _____

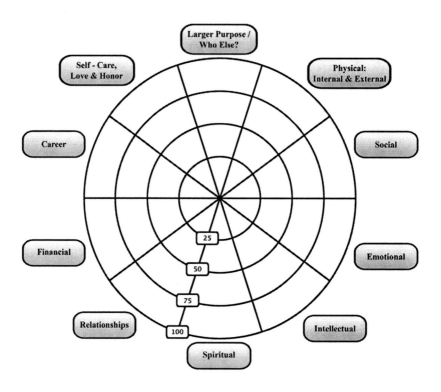

Larger Purpose / Who Else?

Self - Care, Love & Honor

Physical: Internal & External

Career

Social

Financial

Emotional

Relationships

Intellectual

Spiritual

25
50
75
100

Your Assessment Before Your Journey

© 2006 Darlene Braden, db & company.
Permission is granted to copy this page with instructions, provided **no** modifications are made. To purchase the book *What Stops You?*, please go to www.whatstopsyou.com.

Now it's your turn.

Use the following instructions for completing your own Balanced Living Wheel Self-Assessment:

1. Start with the physical category. Place a dot in the center of the pie-slice where you think you are today, 0 being the lowest and 100 being the best you can be (not the world's best, but your best).
2. Refer to "Examples to Consider," on the following pages.
3. **After you have rated a category,** write what stops you from being 100 in that area, on the spaces provided. Be specific.
4. Connect the dots. What shape are you? Are you balanced?
5. What areas are high and what areas are low?
6. What areas do you want to focus on first? It is pretty obvious where you need to improve, eh?

Examples to consider:

Physical:

- How healthy are you?
- What is your ideal weight, your fitness level, flexibility, energy level, etc.?
- Do you experience sickness, pain, or disease?

Rate your answer on the wheel and then answer:

What stops me from being 100 physically? (Possible answers: I eat too much; sleep too much; don't exercise; eat junk food; don't care; don't make physical well-being a priority; manage time poorly.)

_____

_____

_____

_____

Social:

- How many friends do you have, and how comfortable are you around them?
- How comfortable do you feel in a social setting in groups or just one on one?
- Do you feel good about your social life?

Rate your answer on the wheel and then answer:

What stops me from being 100 socially? (Possible answers: I feel uncomfortable in a crowd; don't know what to say; don't have close friends; fear rejection.)

_____
_____
_____
_____

Emotional:

- How emotionally stable are you?
- How level are your moods?
- Are you emotionally comfortable?

Rate your answer on the wheel and then answer:

What stops me from being 100 emotionally? (Possible answers: Fear, anger, trauma, rejection, confusion.)

_____
_____
_____
_____

Intellectual:

- How smart do you think you are in terms of using your potential?
- How well do you use your mind?
- How stimulated do you feel intellectually?

Rate your answer on the wheel and then answer:

What stops me from being 100 intellectually? (Possible answers: I don't read enough; manage time poorly; haven't had enough education; need to learn more about world events; need to make it a priority.)

_____

_____

_____

_____

Spiritual:

- How well do you know and understand your Higher Power?
- How do you feel about your spirituality?
- If you follow a religion, how well are you living what you believe?

Rate your answer on the wheel and then answer:

What stops me from being 100 spiritually? (Possible answers: I don't know who God is; need to pray more; need to serve more; don't care; am confused about religion.)

_____

_____

_____

_____

Relationships:

- How well do you understand and use communication skills?
- Do you forgive, understand, and empathize?
- Do you have rewarding relationships in your life?
- How content are you with the relationships in your life?

Rate your answer on the wheel and then answer:

What stops me from being 100 in my important relationships? (Possible answers: I don't have communication skills, forgiveness, understanding, or patience; I'm selfish; I am too easily distracted by other things.)

_____

_____

_____

_____

Financial:

- Do you have a budget and follow it?
- Do you do the appropriate accounting for your home and business budget?
- How much money do you have? Is it enough?
- Are you disciplined in your spending habits?
- Do you have short and long term savings?
- Do you have investments for the future and retirement plans?

Rate your answer on the wheel and then answer:

What stops me from being 100 financially? (Possible answers: I don't have a financial education; need a budget; don't do accounting; need discipline in spending; have too many accounts receivable.)

_____

_____

_____

_____

Career:

- How much do you enjoy your career, aside from the aspect of money?
- Are you in the career you want to be in?
- Do you feel passion and purpose in your career?
- Does your career fulfill your needs and desires?

Rate your answer on the wheel and then answer:

What stops me from being 100 in my career? (Possible answers: Need to find my passion; am in the wrong profession and don't enjoy what I do; don't enjoy my boss or coworkers; don't know what to do next.)

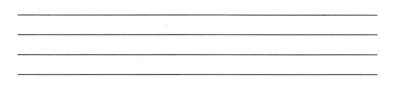

Self-Care:

- How well do you take care of yourself compared with how you take care of your children, pets, etc.?
- Do you honor yourself?
- How much do you love yourself?
- Do you take time for yourself each day, because you are important?
- Are you important?

Rate your answer on the wheel and then answer:

What stops me from being 100 in self-care? (Possible answers: I don't take care of myself as well as I care for my children because I am not as important; don't set boundaries; don't love myself; need to care about filling my cup before always giving too much; don't know who I am.)

_____

_____

_____

_____

Larger Purpose: (Who else is involved? How do I serve?):

- Who else do you consider when making decisions?
- As you live your life, do you consider how you are part of the whole world rather than a separate being? (How do you contribute to the world by simply grocery shopping, reading this book, etc.?)
- How are you involved in service from the heart, not just actions?
- Do you live your life just for yourself, or do you live your life considering the effect you have on others?
- How are you a part of more than just you, every day? (If you don't understand this question, then you most likely will score low in this area.)

Rate your answer on the wheel and then answer:

What stops me from being 100 in my higher purpose? (Possible answers: I don't have enough love for the world; forget that I am part of the bigger whole; am selfish and don't care; don't believe it matters.)

_____

_____

_____

_____

Remember, this is **your** assessment, and 100 on the outer edge of the assessment is the best **you** can be, not the world's best.

How did you do? Did you fill out the wheel and connect the dots? What shape did you create? Does it look like a Pacman, starfish, kite, or egg shape? In my experience, if your shape is small and symmetrical, then you most likely feel depressed or down; if your shape is more like a star, you most likely experience anxiety and confusion. If your shape is large and round, then you feel balanced, and you've done a good job because balance is the goal.

Goal Setting

Now that you have filled out the graph, you can see the areas that are lowest and highest. Let's get started by setting some specific goals to concentrate on and discuss during our sessions. Let's set a personal goal and a business goal.

Personal goals may be in the areas of fitness, social skills, emotional desires, intellectual goals, spiritual goals, relationships, or actions such as having a better golf game.

Professional goals may be in the areas of management, time-management issues, business structure implementation, prospecting and referral gathering, sales process, etc.

Answer the questions in the following exercise.

Goal-Setting Exercise

Think of a goal that you have set before – in fact, many times before – and have not yet achieved. Make your goals very specific and state them positively. Focus on one goal and leave the other goals for next time.

"How do I set a specific goal that is stated positively? Will you give me some examples?" Anna asked.

Here are examples of nonspecific goals.

I want:

- To feel good.
- To not be depressed.
- To not be fat.
- To be happy.
- To have peace.

Here are the same goals, stated positively and specifically. Make sure to consider when you want to achieve the goal, where, and with whom.

What do you want?

I want to feel good:

I want to feel good in my skin at my next reunion. I would know this because I would focus on the other people rather than on what others think of me.

I don't want to be depressed:

I want to feel happiness as I did when I was on vacation at my favorite spot. I want to be able to feel this way every day. I want to have a positive attitude and passion and feel the happiness in my body that I felt on that vacation. I would like to be alert in mind and spirit (rather than depressed).

I don't want to be fat:

I want to lose 7 pounds, be able to run 3 miles without stopping, and have a body fat ratio of 18 percent. That is what I mean by not being fat.

I want to be happy:

I want to be happy around my ex-husband at our daughter's dance recital. I will be able to focus on my daughter and not focus on my ex-husband.

I want to have peace:

I want to feel peaceful, loving, and forgiving at our family reunion when I see my dad for the first time since he abused me verbally.

Before we set your goals, we must first state the problem.

Personal problem:

Anna said, "I am fat."

Professional problem:

Anna said, "I am scared to death to make sales calls. I have a fear of rejection."

Reader's response:

Personal problem:

_____
_____
_____
_____

Professional problem:

_____
_____
_____
_____

Now it is time to set your specific goals.

What do you want?

Anna considered my question for a while and said, "I want to lose 25 pounds in 3 months and get in shape. I want to be a size 6, and I will know that I have achieved my goal when I can fit in my black jeans that I have been saving in the back of my closet."

Anna considered her professional goal and said, "I want to be calm and patient when I make 10 calls per day. I want to feel excited and anticipate the great sales and relationships I will make by placing the calls. I will know I have achieved my goal when I really look forward to using the phones." (Rather than feeling she was going to die before making the calls.)

"So, Anna," I asked, "have you set this goal before? Many times, perhaps millions? Do you know why you have not reached this goal each time?"

She squirmed, made a sarcastic face, and then looked at me seriously. "Darlene, this is why I have really hated myself throughout the years. I can't do it. I just can't. I must admit, though, that I have never set such specific goals, and I am sure that is going to help me. Nonetheless, I have not reached these goals before, so I wonder what might be different this time."

She became more animated and hopeful. She said that if she could find out why she sabotaged herself, she would owe me big time.

Do not be a
GOAL SETTING MANIAC!
Setting goals in all areas at once can be a setup for failure.
Focus on one area at a time.

(To my reader: When setting your goal, be careful NOT to say what you DON'T want. "I don't want to be fat, sick, sad etc." Say what you DO want.)

Reader's response:

What do you want personally? (Specifically, where, when, and with whom?

_____

_____

_____

_____

How will you know you have reached your goal?

_____

_____

_____

_____

What is your motivation for reaching your goal? Why do you want to achieve your goal?

_____

_____

_____

_____

What do you want professionally? (Specifically, where, when, and with whom?)

_____

_____

_____

_____

How will you know you have reached your goal?

_____

_____

_____

_____

What is your motivation to reaching your goal? Why do you want to achieve your goal?

_____

_____

_____

_____

Chapter Four:

A FORK IN THE PATH
Identifying Internal Conflict

Y ou as my reader, along with Anna, may be suffering from self-sabotage in many areas of your life. I will continue to emphasize the fact that in order to find your self-sabotage, you need to know how vitally important it is to recognize where you are **now** in a given area, **before** setting your specific goals. If you were to go on a trip, you would need to know where you were beginning the trek before you planned your  travel agenda. If you were in a mountainous city, or if you were sailing on the ocean, the directions you would follow and the vehicles you would use would be dramatically different.

Now that you have set your goals, let's look at the formula for change and success.

The NLP formula for change is:

Present State + Resources = Desired State.

In other words, the order of getting what you want is:

1. Ask: "Where am I now?" (Present state)
2. Ask: "What is my goal?" (Desired state)
3. Ask: "What stops me from reaching my goal?" (Diagnosis)
4. Make appropriate changes. (Resources)

Simple! Now before you get too excited, we are never done assessing. The Balanced Living Wheel Self-Assessment is the first step in determining **what stops you** from reaching your goals; sometimes that's all you need. However, to be thorough, let's continue looking at where you are now, and discover any internal conflicts. Understanding conflicts is hugely important in becoming the person you really want to be.

As we proceed you will be amazed at how common conflicts are. What specific conflicts stop you from achieving your goals?

Discovering Your Personal and Professional Self-Sabotage

You can use a variety of ways to find out how you are sabotaging yourself. The first and easiest way is to acknowledge the daily conflicts that you experience. Conflicts occur when part of your mind wants one thing, and part of your mind wants something else. When this happens, there is a great deal of confusion. This state is very uncomfortable and, depending on the degree of the conflict, it can be painful with severe ramifications. When we act out of one side of the mind based on actions that we have suppressed, we may do something inappropriate and damaging.

When we act out of the **other** side of the mind, the opportunity may arise when this side reacts as well. In this state of mind, there is a lack of peace, to put it simply.

Acknowledge the daily conflicts that you experience.

You may recall Jiminy Cricket in the movie *Pinocchio*. Jiminy Cricket is the small cricket representing Pinocchio's conscience. The wolf and his friends constantly persuade Pinocchio to do things that are wrong. When Pinocchio begins doing something naughty, Jiminy Cricket jumps on Pinocchio's shoulder and speaks up, telling him what not to do. At times Pinocchio listens, and other times he does not. He constantly struggles whether to listen to the wolf or to listen to Jiminy. Jiminy has to be very persistent with Pinocchio to get him to listen.

What conflicts do you have?

Here are some examples of both personal and professional internal conflicts:

- Part of me wants to be good and serve God, yet part of me is mad at God because…
- Part of me wants to read this book and learn more, yet part of me feels that it won't do any good, or I'm too busy.
- Part of me wants to be a business person, and part of me wants to be a stay-at-home mom/dad.
- Part of me likes my coworkers, and part of me does not.
- Part of me wants to exercise, but part of me wants to rest and eat.
- Part of me loves my spouse, but part of me wants to find a new partner.
- Part of me wants to get up early and get a lot done, but part of me wants to sleep in.
- Part of me wants to start my own company, but part of me wants to work for someone else and leave all the administrative stuff to them.
- Part of me wants to go to the networking meeting to get new clients, and part of me is afraid to present my product.

Anna started squirming in the chair. "Wow, you nailed it. You are right! Only part of me wanted to call you and meet for lunch; the other part was scared you would be disappointed in me. Part of me wanted to wear a skirt, and part of me wanted to wear a business jacket to look more professional. **I had millions of conflicts before noon!"**

It is common to be in conflict most of the time. Most people walk around in conflict to some degree or another. As you think about your day, list the conflicts that have occurred just today. Focus only on today. Let's start simply so you can begin the learning curve of conflict awareness.

List today's conflicts that you are aware of:

_____
_____
_____
_____

How did you do? Did you notice some splits in what you want and where you are? In a later chapter, we will learn what to do with the conflicts. The ultimate goal is to have **all of your parts in agreement** – for example, when **all of you** wants to get up early and get things done; **your heart, mind, body, and spirit** want to rise with the early sun and be productive.

Here are examples of general categories of conflicts. See if you can point out the category that you are experiencing.

- **Self vs. Others:** Either I please others, or I please myself.
- **External vs. Internal:** Part of me cares about what others think, and part makes choices based on what feels good.

- **Good vs. Bad:** I want to be a committed husband, but part of me wants to go out and party with another woman that I am attracted to.
- **Should vs. Don't want to:** I should do the filing, but most of me wants to watch TV.

Keep in mind that it is common to have more than two conflicts about the same thing and at the same time. If this is so, the problem is more complex, and you may need a coach or therapist to guide you through specific techniques.

This week, continue noticing and writing down your conflicts. Which conflicts are stopping you from your goals? What are you going to do about it?

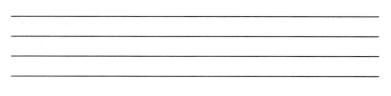

Chapter Five:

GETTING STALLED ALONG THE WAY

Seeing Hidden Intents
That Keep You Stuck

There are a variety of ways to find the self-sabotage you are experiencing. Conflicts are one way. Did you find some conflicts inside you, in the last section? You may have already solved your issue. If so, pick another goal; if not, let's keep going. Look at the following questions and review them. I will guide you through your answers later in the chapter.

First, think of the personal and professional goals that you set in chapter 3. (Anna's goals were to lose 25 pounds in 3 months and to make 10 cold calls a day while feeling comfortable.)

Since you CAN'T find **what stops you** until you have set a specific goal, don't continue reading this book until you have done so. You may want to refer to chapter 3, again, and complete the goal setting exercises.

As you think of the personal and professional goals that you set, consider the following questions. There will be a place provided to fill out the answers later.

What specific goal do I want?

1. **What stops me from achieving my goal?**
2. **What part of myself objects to achieving this goal?**
3. **What is the positive intent of not achieving this goal?** (Why might I not really want it after all?)
4. **What would happen if I really achieved my goal, magically, right now?** Could any negative consequences happen if I achieved my goal now? Am I sure? (Take time to think about this.)

Let me give you an example of a negative consequence. A client came into my office wanting to get rid of his allergies to wheat, which made him suffer all year long with sneezing, swelling, and coughing. He reported how many food items had wheat in them and how he had educated himself about ingredients and food labels. He had studied wheat replacements and alternative foods in depth.

I asked him what his life would be like and what it would feel and look like **if** he responded to wheat in a healthy way.

He described in detail all the freedom he would experience, such as breathing freely, focusing on a larger menu because he could eat more types of food, and having more time to be productive.

I then asked him, "Is there anything bad about

overcoming this allergy and having an appropriate response to wheat?"

His immediate response was, "Absolutely not!"

Again I asked him to **take time and ponder** if there were any negative consequences that could take place if he magically had his goal right now. Was there anything that he might possibly lose that he did not want to lose by **not** being allergic to wheat?

He then paused and said, "Well, it sure is a conversation piece to have my face swell up and share war stories with other allergy sufferers. And I hate to admit that on Thursdays for the past few years, my mom has brought me her special soup to help me feel better. I really enjoy her visits. If I were not allergic to wheat, then I imagine that I would not have this special relationship with my mom."

(I just love it when Anna's animated face portrays that she is enjoying my stories. She is very demonstrative as she replies that she "gets it.")

Anna said, "All righty, then, I understand. That was a flippin' struggle because it seems it would just be totally good to not have your face all swollen up. Now I do get it. I'm guessing that lots of people have negative consequences that they are not aware of right away. Am I right?"

Please use the space below or write in your own workbook to answer the following important questions. Take time to ponder and search for the answers that seem right. Understand that there is a learning curve to self-discovery. Be nice and patient with yourself.

Personal Goal:

1. What specific goal do I want? (Goal you set in chapter 3.)

(Anna said, "To lose 25 pounds in 3 months.")

_____

_____

_____

_____

2. What stops me from achieving my personal goal?

(Anna said, "I eat too much, and that is a fact. I love greasy foods and I love sugar. I crave the extra-full feeling I get when I am done with a meal. I love the atmosphere of restaurants, and I like to pamper myself with food. It is the only real enjoyment I ever have.")

_____

_____

_____

_____

3. What part of me objects to achieving my personal goal?

(Anna said, "The part of me that does not want to suffer, starve, and be lonely.")

_____

_____

_____

_____

4. What is the positive intent of not having what I really want?

(Anna said, "If I don't have to worry about being thin, then I get to eat, eat, and eat what I want. Also, fat repels people emotionally and physically, so I don't have to worry about getting too close to people.")

_____
_____
_____
_____

5. If I magically attained my goal right now, how would this possibly make me uncomfortable?
For example: My client who was allergic to wheat might lose the nurturing relationship with his mom.

(Anna continued, "If I were thin, it would put pressure on me to eat better. If I were thin and beautiful, I might not be as committed to Jake because I would get more attention from other men.")

_____
_____
_____
_____

So what I <u>really</u> want is: (Your goal may or may not have shifted.) _____

_____

Professional Goal:

1. What specific goal do I want? (Goal you set in chapter 3.)

(Anna responds, "To be able to comfortably make business calls each day.")

_____

_____

_____

_____

2. What stops me from achieving my professional goal?

(Anna said, "I am afraid of the phones because I hate rejection from the person on the other line.")

_____

_____

_____

_____

3. What part of me objects to achieving my professional goal?

(Anna said, "If I spend too much time on professional pursuits, I won't have time for my boyfriend.")

_____

_____

_____

_____

4. What is the positive intent of not having what I really want? For example: What is good about feeling bad? What is good about not achieving my goal? (Answering this question will reveal your secondary gain or a possible unconscious reason for not achieving your goal.)

(Anna's response: "I can have more free time and not have that horrible stomach feeling. Besides, if my stomach hurts, some of my colleagues will make the calls for me. I can relax and not worry about bugging or offending people.")

_____

_____

_____

_____

5. If I magically attained my goal right now, how would this possibly make me uncomfortable?

(Anna said, "If I were comfortable on the phone and not afraid of rejection, then I would be successful in sales. As much as I thought I wanted it, I guess there is a part of me that thinks that Jake would be intimidated, and then he wouldn't take care of me.")

_____

_____

_____

_____

So what I really want is: (Your goal may or may not have shifted.) _____

_____

Now you can see and feel that one of the main reasons you have not achieved your goal is that part of you doesn't want to achieve it. How simple is that? Many therapists, coaches, and motivational speakers would have you say to your objecting parts, "Go away or be gone." They would tell you not to listen to these parts. They would have you tell the part to be quiet, or better yet, to "shut up." Or the coach may propose that you try to just blow up your objecting parts to get rid of them.

I will show you that the opposite is true. Let us acknowledge these objecting parts. We will invite these objecting parts to come forward and speak so that we can assist them. If we invited our enemies to talk and speak their minds, it would defuse our enemies, would it not?

We will refer back to this section later. Keep your notebook handy as we continue.

One of the main reasons that you haven't achieved your goal is that part of you doesn't want to achieve it.

Chapter Six:

FOLLOWING EMOTIONAL CLUES

Hidden Messages of Your "Negative" Emotions

"Anna," I said, "let's now acknowledge some of the **emotional parts** of your mind." Most individuals have some or all of the following emotional parts:

- **Angry part**
- **Sad part**
- **Happy part**
- **Hopeful part**
- **Fearful part**
- **Rejected part**
- **Glad part**
- **Lonely part**
- **Revengeful part**
- **Resentful part**

Most people have all of these emotional parts somewhere inside their minds. Each emotional part can be manifested only **one at a time,** while the others are suppressed. Right? Are you with me?

This next part is awesome, yet not everyone will be aware of what I am about to ask. If that is the case for you, then be open to awareness and come back in a day or so, when your awareness has been heightened, and reread the section.

Now, if your ready, sit back and relax. Be aware of your breathing, and prepare to notice what is happening inside you. Reflect back on last week. What emotional parts did you feel?

It is time for self-awareness. Where in your body do you feel anger – the head, stomach, heart, etc.? Where do you feel sad, happy, hopeful, fearful, lonely, or rejected?

List **where in your body** you feel each emotion. Think back to the **most recent time you have felt these emotions.** For reasons of discovery, fully relive the experience in your mind.

Anger: _____

Sadness: _____

Happiness: _____

Hope: _____

Fear: _____

Rejection: _____

Gladness: _____

Loneliness: _____

Revenge: _____

Resentment: _____

How did you do? Were you aware that anger may be a burning in your throat or pressing in your chest? Maybe loneliness was a pressure or hollow feeling in your heart or an empty feeling in your stomach. What did you notice? Realize that each individual experiences emotions in different places in their bodies, and there is no wrong location.

In the preceding list, circle the emotions that you experienced. Next to the word, rate the emotional intensity on a scale of 1 to 5 (1 = the least intense; 5 = the most intense). Write the intensity (1 to 5) next to the word based on how strong the feelings were.

Please read this slowly and carefully: The emotions that you rated a 5 usually have an opposing emotional part. If you put a 5 for anger, then its possible opposing part would be love or empathy. Those you rated lower than 5 do not have an obvious opposing emotional part, so we will need to search for the opposing part.

All of a sudden, Anna grabbed her stomach and leaned over. She was still and lifeless. After quite a while, she sat up and stared blankly at the wall behind me, and then tears began to gather in her gaze. "Wow," she said slowly. "I feel so lonely, fearful, and abandoned. I had a hideous memory of the past, and I feel as if it is real and happening right now. I feel helpless and frozen."

I gave her empathy and assured her that I was by her side. I told her to verbally thank her stomach for this communication and feedback. I explained that her stomach had feelings that were locked inside and that we would put these feelings on hold for now and acknowledge them later.

I had her break her state of mind by walking out to the street and noticing all the smells of pending winter before she came back inside.

She entered the office ready to move on as long as we would revisit this issue later. I assured her that we would.

All feelings are manifested somewhere in the physical body.

Now let's look at other parts that you have. You have a head, a heart, a body, a gut, and a soul. It is very interesting that these parts can be completely out of touch with each other and attempt to operate individually, which manifests as **self-sabotage.**

The parts are:

- **Head = Logic**
- **Heart = Passion**
- **Body = Physical feelings**
- **Gut = Deep, unconscious "gut feeling"**

- **Spirit = Sense of more; sense of who we are if we imagine we do not have a body**

Let's use a relationship example to explain how the parts can oppose each other and manifest as a conflict. On a scale from 1 to 10, let's ask Tiffany how much she loves Alex.

She says, "With my **heart,** oh, a 10. I love him to death. I care about him very much. If he is sad, I am tortured. I love to see him smile.

"With my **body,** oh ya, a 10. He is the sexiest guy I know. Oh my.

"With my **gut,** just a 4 because I just get the feeling that this is just a short-term relationship.

"With my **soul,** an 8. We love to be together, and I am attracted to his spirit.

"Well, with my **head,** about a 1, because you see, he is in prison right now for killing small children and – um, well – he didn't mean to, and he is really a good person underneath it all. He is working things out, but I don't know how our relationship will work if he is locked up for life."

Anna laughed and said, "I think Tiffany has a conflict!"

Here is another example of Suzie and Dan.

Suzie said, "With my **head,** I love Dan a 10. His family is like mine. We both are in the same business, and we both want kids.

"With my **heart,** I love him about a 4. I don't really know him well enough to know his deep feelings.

"With my **body,** I love him a 4. I am OK kissing him, but I am a bit too tall for him, and he has funny hands. You know, he kind of stinks a little bit, too."

Anna and I laughed as I continued the example.

"With my **gut,** I love him a 2. I just have this gut feeling that as good as it seems, we may not be together for very long.

"With my **soul,** I love him a 9. I can imagine our souls flying around together without bodies and feeling good together.

"Anna," I said, "You can see why most people do not answer a resounding 'yes' when asked if they love someone. With this rating scale, you can clearly see if you have a physical relationship or an internal relationship or a combination. Take the time to understand why your spirit objects; why your head objects. Slow down and honor the parts of you that object.

"By the way, your unconscious mind is not very smart, at least not in a logical way. Your unconscious just reacts. Its only purpose is to preserve the species; to preserve you. Since it does not know any better, it just reacts to situations the best it knows how."

Your unconscious mind is not very smart, at least not in a logical way.

Anna started chuckling out loud. She began listing all 5,000 of her past boyfriends and all the conflicts and rating her feelings about each guy. She had "kind of" loved Clay, Tom, Skip, Andy, Rob, and on and on. She realized she was never all 10s on any relationship. We started laughing about Beck's funny toes and how they lowered his rating. We began to get too giddy to continue. We called it a day, and she left with greater insight. She left murmuring, "No wonder, no wonder, conflict city going on inside of me. Geeze Louise!"

Chapter Seven:

CLIMBING THE PYRAMID OF THOUGHT

Understanding How Your Brain Works

T he Pyramid of Thought" is based on Robert Dilts' original model, "The Neurological Levels," which is an adaptation of Gregory Bateson's notion of "Logical Levels." Bateson is a systems theorist psychologist. "The Neurological Levels" is a model that relates Bateson's levels of processing to the nervous system. Gregory Bateson points out that human beings process information at differing levels of physiology. The depth of neurology that is activated when a person is processing at the identity level, for instance, is much deeper than the level of neurology that is required to move an arm. Based on Dilts' and Bateson's work, I refer to the following levels or layers throughout this book.

Purpose / Mission
For whom? For What?
(Beyond self, aura, morphagenic field)

Identity
Who am I?
(Immune system / Endocrine system)

Beliefs & Values
Why?
(Autonomic nervous system / unconscious responses)

Skills
How?
(Cortical system)

Actions
What?
(Pyramidal nervous system / motor system - conscious actions)

Environment
Where, When?
(Peripheral nervous system / Sensation - reflex reactions)

The Pyramid of Thought

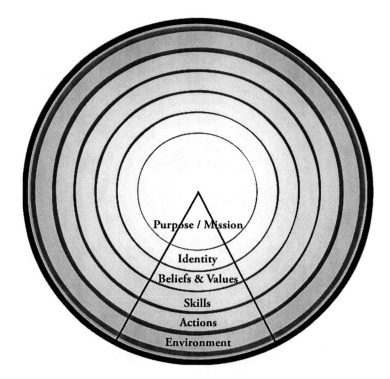

I had Anna refer to the onion picture. As the graphic shows, we see that the levels of the pyramid are like layers of an onion. **The pyramid represents a wedge** of the onion or the layers of the neurology inside your body.

Please refer to the next example of "The Pyramid of Thought" that describes each layer in more detail.

In the following graphic, we start at the top of the pyramid; we acknowledge that it represents the center of us as human beings. It relates to our sense of who we are. It represents our purpose, our spirit and soul. Spiritual-level experiences have to do with our sense of being part of something more than ourselves on a very deep and connected level. Neurologically, it represents our aura or countenance.

Purpose / Mission

For whom? For What?

(Beyond self, aura, morphagenic field)

At the Purpose/Mission level, we ask: "For whom?" and "For what?"

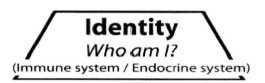

Identity

Who am I?

(Immune system / Endocrine system)

At the Identity level, we ask: "Who am I?"

As we look at the Identity level, above, we see that our Identity is located close to the top and almost in our center. Identity represents who we feel that we are. Neurologically, this level represents the immune system and endocrine system. It represents deep, life-sustaining actions such as kidney and pancreas functions. We ask questions such as:

- **Who am I?**
- **Am I worth it?**
- **Do I deserve success?**

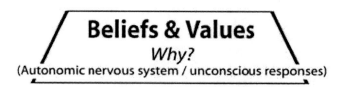

At the Belief level, we ask: "Why?"

The Beliefs & Values level is just a small distance from our center. What do we believe about ourselves, others, and the world in general? Neurologically, this level activates the autonomic nervous system functions, such as heart rate, pupil dilation, and unconscious responses.

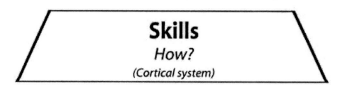

At the Skills level, we ask: "How?"

Skills are the ability to be capable, and they are not as hard wired as Identity. Neurologically, the cortical system is engaged. The cortical system controls semiconscious actions such as eye movements, posture, etc.

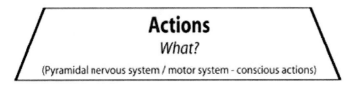

At the Actions level, we ask: "What?"

The actions level is referred to as the motor system. It engages the pyramidal nervous system, which refers to conscious action. Actions and behaviors are simply what we do or do not do, such as brushing our teeth or picking up a pencil.

At the Environment level, we ask: "Where and when?"

On the outside is the external world, the environment. What is going on in the world around you, and how are you responding to the environmental stimuli? Neurologically, the peripheral nervous system is engaged, causing sensations and reflex reactions.

I recommend that you study the pyramid for a moment. Look at it and see that each level refers to a different level of physical neurology; the deeper in, the more neurology is invested, so it is harder to change the inner levels than the outer levels. For example, it is more difficult to shift a deeply wired belief than a simple external behavior.

Now we'll continue finding your sabotage. We will review each level specifically in terms of your personal and professional experiences.

- If you have friends who are constantly asking "Why" questions such as "Why me?", you know that their minds are operating in the area of **Mental Processes.**
- If they are asking "How" questions such as "How does that work?", they are operating in the areas of **Skills or Actions.**

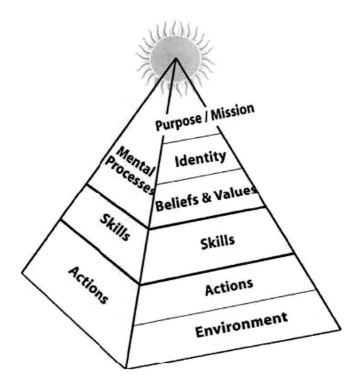

Look at the pyramid from a different angle. Notice the three dimensional view of the pyramid considering how **actions, skills, and mental processes** are categories of the pyramid of thought.

"Anna," I said, "as we review the triangle, consider the goal that you have set for yourself at the beginning of the book."

Have your specific goal in mind and ask this question: "What stops me from achieving my goal now?" Consider either your business goal and/or personal goal.

Chapter Eight:

STEEP SLOPES, CALM MEADOWS

Recognizing the Environment's Influence

S o what stops you from achieving your goal now? Is it the environment? Where and when do you do what you do? Is your environment working for you so that you can achieve what you desire?

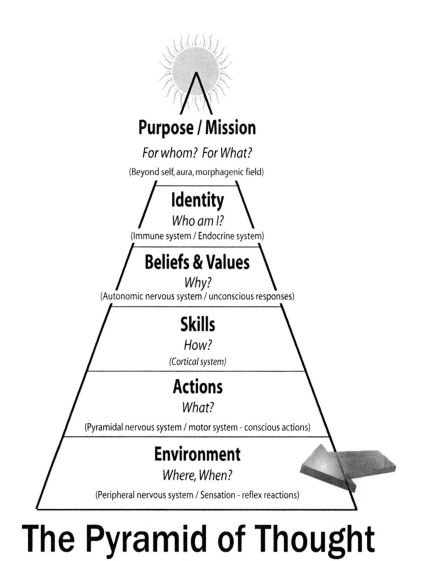

The Pyramid of Thought

We will begin at the bottom of the pyramid, to find your self-sabotage, and then move up the levels in each of the following chapters. The following lists will seem to be negative comments only, yet they are possible excuses for **what stops you** from success. They are just examples. You may identify with some or perhaps none of the examples on the list.

What stops you on the Environment level, if anything?

Personal Examples:

- My gym is too far away.
- I don't have running shoes.
- My leg is broken so I can't work out.
- My golf clubs are missing.
- My vacuum belt has ripped.
- I get up too late.
- I don't take time for relationships.

Where in the environment are you stopped? There may be nothing that stops you, so you are ready to go to the next level. If something in the environment is stopping you, write it down.

(Anna allowed her environment to stop her from losing 25 pounds because her gym membership had lapsed and she did not have any workout shoes.)

I am stopped from achieving my personal goal on the Environment level because:

_____

_____

_____

_____

Professional Examples:

- My cubicle is too small.
- I live in the wrong state (for example, I sell snow skis in Florida).
- The people in my office talk too much, and I don't have a door on my office.
- My invoices got lost.
- My bills are late because I don't have stamps.
- My watch stopped, so I have been late all day.

What stops you on the Environment level in business, if anything?

(Anna was stopped on the Environment level from making 10 cold calls per day because her phone line had a bit of static on it.)

_____

__Hint for Changing__
__Environmental Sabotage__: Find a way to change it. If you can't change your state of mind, change your state (Utah or California, for example). Now be careful. Before you change your state and move to Alabama, finish reading this book.

_____

There is so much talk about changing your state of mind and accepting what is. Changing your state of mind is very powerful! Yet, we only have the ability to change ourselves, and we cannot change others. Wouldn't it be awesome if you could just change someone else? Life would be so easy. For example: "Hey, give me all your money. Hey, talk nice to me. Hey, tell me I am wonderful. And, hey, tell me that you are sorry." Well, since we can't have that, what do we want? **We want personal empowerment.** Each of us wants to understand and control our thoughts and actions. We can have more appropriate power and control when we focus and take action to heal ourselves with what is.

Sometimes, however, it is appropriate to take action and change our environment. At times it is appropriate to just simply sell the van, change the office location, and fire the obnoxious secretary. It is great to take external **action.**

It is important to review the rest of the triangle before changing too much of our external world as the higher levels affect our feelings about our environment.

Anna came to her session all excited that she had fixed the static on her phone lines. She was ready to try her calls each morning. She also stated that she had made it a priority to renew her gym membership and purchase workout shoes. She was on her way to success.

Along with Anna, answer the following question in the areas of both **personal and professional.**

What immediate actions will you take?

_____

_____

_____

_____

Chapter Nine:

ANNA PUTS ONE FOOT IN FRONT OF THE OTHER
Taking Appropriate Actions for Success

W hat is an **action?** An action is a behavior that is observable and can be seen by others. For example, I talk; I walk. An **action** is what you do or what you don't do.

Please look at the pyramid as we focus on the **Actions** level.

The Pyramid of Thought

Personal Examples:

- I eat too fast and too much.
- I love sugar too much.
- I use my right hand when I swing my golf clubs.
- I throw the ball too far to the left.
- I talk loudly.
- I read too long each evening.
- I dance with two left feet.
- I cook occasionally.
- I fidget.
- I sleep a lot.

(Anna was stopped from losing 25 pounds on the **Actions** level because she ate too much and too fast, didn't notice or count what she ate, and didn't exercise at all.)

Professional Examples:

- I don't make enough cold calls per day.
- I talk too fast when I present my material.
- I forget to take my business cards with me.
- I don't give my 30-second business introduction often enough.
- I don't plan my day.
- I forget to request referrals.
- I don't set daily and weekly goals.
- I don't review my sales presentation.
- I submit my invoices late.
- I market inefficiently.

What stops you from achieving your goal on the Actions level? (Personal and professional.)

_____

_____

_____

_____

Is what stops you something that you simply do or don't do? Explain. (Personal and professional.)

_____

_____

_____

_____

(Anna was stopped from making 10 calls a day because she watched TV until it was too late to call.)

Here is one of my funny jokes. (I really have a lot of funny jokes.) This guy goes to see his doctor because he is quite concerned about his sore hip. Every time he brings his knee way up to his chest and then lowers his foot quickly to the floor, he hears a huge pop, and it really hurts. The pop is so loud that the neighbors can probably hear it.

The doctor comes into the room and asks the guy to show him what he does to make his hip pop and hurt. The man stands up with energy to show the doctor his newfound malady. He brings his knee right up to his chest and quickly lowers his foot to the floor. Sure enough, pop. The doctor says, "Wow, that really pops!"

The doctor leaves the room to consult his colleagues. After what seems like an eternity, the doctor returns. He comes up to the man, looks him in the eye, and says, "I have met with some renowned orthopedic doctors. I explained that you raise your knee and lower your leg quickly and hear a pop. The consensus of the panel is that the way to alleviate the pop and pain is to ... **just stop doing that!**" **Ha!**

Hints for Changing Your Sabotage on an Action/Behavioral Level:

Just do it! Or just stop doing that!

Action change is about commitment, follow-through, and personal accountability. If you are stopped on the Actions level only, **then take action or stop some unneeded action.** The fact is that you are most likely stopped in one or more of the levels above **Actions.** If not, then you will have your goal shortly by taking action.

You have to love Anna. She came into my office today a bit more serious about all this action-changing stuff. She reported that she was eating more slowly, she had gotten a calorie counter, and she had started working out at her gym four or five times per week. She also learned that making her business calls **before** she watched TV worked well – and then she got to relax afterwards with her favorite show.

Answer both personal and professional:

What actions will you take?

_____

_____

_____

_____

Chapter Ten:

LEARNING AS
YOU GO
Developing and Practicing Skills to Become More Proficient

R eview the triangle as we progress up the layers. Notice how the layers are separate yet connected to each other. Notice that the farther up we go, the harder things are to change. The neurology is deeper as we progress upward and inward.

Skills and abilities measure how well you do a task. They are how competent and skilled you are.

Purpose / Mission
For whom? For What?
(Beyond self, aura, morphagenic field)

Identity
Who am I?
(Immune system / Endocrine system)

Beliefs & Values
Why?
(Autonomic nervous system / unconscious responses)

Skills
How?
(Cortical system)

Actions
What?
(Pyramidal nervous system / motor system - conscious actions)

Environment
Where, When?
(Peripheral nervous system / Sensation - reflex reactions)

The Pyramid of Thought

Are you stopped on the Skills level?

Personal Examples:

- I don't play the violin very well.
- I can't run 5 miles.
- I have a very hard time saying "I'm sorry."
- I eat faster than other people do.
- I can't hit the baseball over the fence.
- I never remember to brush my teeth at noon.
- I can't seem to remember my new neighbor's name.
- It seems like every time I back out of my driveway, I run over the sprinkler heads.

(Anna was stopped on the Skills level from losing 25 pounds because she did not know about nutrition and she did not know how to exercise appropriately.)

Professional Examples:

- I can't prospect.
- I'm shy and unable to ask potential clients for their business.
- I am unable to close a sale.
- I'm too nervous to call referrals.
- I'm unable to manage my team because they laugh at my requests.
- I don't have a script and I don't know what to say.
- I manage tasks very poorly.
- I don't know how to organize my office.

- I forget to set appointments.
- I don't know enough information to answer my customers' questions.

(Anna was stopped on the Skills level from making 10 business calls per day because she did not know **what to do. She did not have a script**, and she stuttered and stammered when she talked.)

How well do you accomplish a task? At the Skills level, there is an element of competence that becomes natural as you practice. If you are stuck at this level, I recommend that you model others who are successful in the area you are interested in. How do they do a task? Ask them; model them; and practice, practice, practice.

Hint:
If you are stuck on the Skills level, traditional seminars are wonderful. School, continuing education, lessons, and practice will increase your abilities. Learn more; implement behavior; and practice, practice, practice.

I remember when I was in sixth grade, and Marci and I would have a Friday night sleepover. Those were the years that contact lenses were hard and hideously uncomfortable. They were really difficult to put in because it just seemed weird to put pieces of light brown glass in our eyes. Well, Mom and the doctor said that it was OK to put pieces of glass in our eyes, so Marci and I went into the bathroom and began to practice putting in and taking out our scratchy contacts, over and over, until it was easy. In and out they went, and sure enough, after an hour or so, we could do it without the mirror. Both of us learned to be great at this newfound skill.

When we practice a skill, our neurology begins to shift, and the new "habit" becomes natural. When we go outside our comfort zone by repeatedly practicing a new skill, our comfort zone grows. It is so great to see and feel our comfort zones grow!

Years ago, I was a district manager and sales representative for a well-known cosmetic company. I remember making reorder calls to my customers. I would dread the evenings when I knew I had to – and I mean had to – go into my office, flip through the last month's orders, and call all the scary people and ask them if they wanted more cleansing lotion.

I remember getting really bugged that it bugged me. I was upset that I felt nervous and made excuses. So, I set a goal for myself that I would call as many clients as it took until I was comfortable. Sure enough, after about an hour, I became more comfortable. Then the next night the fear came back a bit, and I would call and call again until I was comfortable. Some customers said, "No, I don't like your product." Some said that very soon they would need to reorder. Others said, "The cleansing cream gives me zits." Some wanted their money back, but most people wanted more product. I realized that the voice on the other end of the phone was a real person, and I was learning to enjoy the relationship I was building with my clients. At last, **I looked forward** to making reorder calls to my friends on the other end of the phone line, and I was completely comfortable.

I was stopped on the Skills level, and the fix was to just do it and practice, practice, practice.

Now, what if after all the practice of calling, I was still afraid of making these calls? Referencing the pyramid, I may realize that I was stuck on one of the layers **above** the level of Skills. Then I would need to discover more about my **beliefs** and **identity**.

Anna reported that on the Skills personal level, she had hired a personal trainer for five sessions to give her the basic knowledge about nutrition and the appropriate way to exercise so that her workouts were effective. On a professional Skills level, we worked on her calling script. The script went something like this:

Script for getting referrals:

"_____ (name), I need your help. In my business, I work by referrals to build my clientele. **Who** do you know that **might possibly** like more information about _____ (your business's service)? **Who else?** And who else?

"_____ (name), what I would like to do is call your referrals, ask them some quick questions about their needs, tell them a sentence about what I can do for them, and then, if there is a fit, we can schedule an appointment to gather more information. If there isn't a fit, then I will thank them for their time. Fair enough?"

The idea here is to set up the get-together and **not educate them about your product yet.** (I recommend calling the meeting a "get-together" rather than an appointment or meeting.)

Script for calling referrals:

"Hi, my name is Anna. Do you have a quick minute? I got your name from _____ (source). He/she said that you were open to new, creative ideas about _____(industry). Is that right? What I would like to do is get together with you and spend about 30 minutes asking you specific questions about your needs. I will then briefly let you know what our company is about and what we can do for you. If there is a fit, great; we can do business. If not, I will thank you for your time. Is that fair?"

After Anna practiced the script many times, she stopped stuttering and began to "own" her script.

In most industries there are trainers that can help you get scripted. When you own the script it will give you confidence and help you have appropriate control over the conversation. This will lead you through the process of prospecting, the presentation, and asking for the client's business.

Keep in mind I have only shared referral scripts with you. There are many specific scripts available per your industry.

What actions will you take? (Personally and professionally.)

_____

_____

_____

_____

What skills do you need to develop and practice? (Personally and professionally.)

_____

_____

_____

_____

_____

BIG HINT:
To create lasting change, you must
recognize and shift to the level ABOVE
where you are stuck.

_____

Chapter Eleven:

I THINK I CAN
I THINK I CAN'T
*Shifting Gears by Shifting
Limiting Beliefs*

This section on **beliefs** is a very important one. We will spend a lot of time here. When we are searching for personal or professional sabotage, it is quite common to discover the sabotage on the Beliefs & Values level. Beliefs are more deeply wired than skills and actions. I absolutely love the topic of beliefs because they are so powerful and drive our actions. **When we understand HOW,** it is quite simple to change limiting beliefs.

Many of my clients formed limiting beliefs during perceived or real traumatic episodes in childhood. They try to survive or keep sane by masking these feelings, burying their feelings alive, and hoping to mummify the issues. Too bad, so sad; this does not work.

Purpose / Mission
For whom? For What?
(Beyond self, aura, morphagenic field)

Identity
Who am I?
(Immune system / Endocrine system)

Beliefs & Values
Why?
(Autonomic nervous system / unconscious responses)

Skills
How?
(Cortical system)

Actions
What?
(Pyramidal nervous system / motor system - conscious actions)

Environment
Where, When?
(Peripheral nervous system / Sensation - reflex reactions)

The Pyramid of Thought

Beliefs are awfully hard wired in the neurology. If this were not true, then if my friend said, "I believe the world is scary," all I would need to say to help her change her thought pattern would be, "No, it's not. The world is safe and fun to discover." My friend would then just say, "Oh my heck, thanks so much. Now I believe the world is fun to discover!" Hard-wired beliefs can be limiting, yet they keep us from being too gullible, which could be very limiting by itself.

Question: Is a belief real?

- **Yes**
- **No**

What was your answer? Are beliefs real or not real? I imagine that part of you wanted to say "yes" and part of you wanted to say "no."

The perceived answer is: Beliefs are real to the person who is experiencing them. Fair enough? For example, if you believe you are not important, then sure enough, the belief will seem true to you.

The actual answer is that beliefs are not real. Let me explain.

Anna was listening intently, so I continued to explain.

Let's define "real." Something real in this world is documented by science, and it is tangible and testable. The statement "This is a chair" is not a belief. "I believe it is a big, useful chair" or "a beautiful chair" or "a dumb chair" is a belief or perception.

Because our perceptions are not real, we are all walking around with our own reality in our own little private worlds with all our meanings and stories about ourselves, others, and beliefs about the world.

REAL: Something that can be documented by science and is tangible and testable.

So really, not much is real. Even memories of our past are not real. If a football was in the middle of the room and someone moved it, it would no longer be here, would it?

We may have a memory of the football, but it is not real at all now. So if this is the case, why do past events still seem so real right now? Why do you feel rejected or sad or traumatized just by remembering an event? If it is not real and is in the past and is not there anymore, why does one feel the emotion years, decades, and possibly a half century later?

The answer is quite simple. Our experiences cause us to attach meanings and beliefs to the stimulus. The belief causes a physical feeling in the body, and this feeling is embedded deeply inside us. The Eastern school of thought contends that the memory of a feeling is coded in our cell memory, DNA, and muscle memory. For this reason, we must address not only the mind but also the body and the spirit. Some of my colleagues believe that the spirit is where we code all information that is coded in the body.

Our experiences cause us to attach meanings and beliefs to the stimulus.

Energy workers, massage therapists, and healers know that body work is essential to move toxins and positive and negative energy. It is important to move the memory out of the body.

Catharsis of any kind – be it crying, talking, or visualizing – moves this memory around. Some memories are so "stuck" that people will search for years for something to help them.

Are you still with me, or did I lose you? I remember all this stuff being weird at one point in my life. (Weird is that which you do not understand.) Now it is part of my day, part of my practice, and part of who I am. There is power in knowledge and practice. My dad always said, "Wise men seek wise counsel." How true that is. I commend you for reaching out to learn more about how your beliefs have sabotaged your success.

There are three distinct categories of beliefs:

1. **Beliefs about self.**
2. **Beliefs about others.**
3. **Beliefs about the world in general.**

As we probe more deeply inside our feelings and emotions, we recognize that the English language falls terribly short in helping us express what we feel and experience. One of my clients once said that she felt as though she had to cram her feelings into the English language. Sometimes there are no words to describe how we feel.

Beliefs are equations.

I believe that I am ugly = No one will like me = I'm not acceptable = I'm useless = I don't exist = I'm going to die.

I believe that I am not lovable = I will be lonely the rest of my life = I'm not important = I'm helpless and alone = I will die.

I believe that I am dumb = I will be poor = I won't survive = I will die.

Most limiting beliefs eventually can be equated with death. No wonder the limiting belief of being unlovable is so drastically painful.

It is not your life that causes problems; it is the meaning you make of your life that causes problems.

Humans are meaning-making machines that make meaning constantly and continually. We all make meaning from every conversation we have, everyone we meet, things that happen around us, and things that don't happen. We form our own perceptions and perspectives all day long as though our way of thinking is a tangible reality.

Life Makes Meaning

During your life, you have had both positive and negative experiences. As you live through your day-to-day routine experiences, you continually associate meaning with those experiences. Beliefs are formed as you develop and grow, beginning from your conception and continuing throughout your life.

Your brain codes both logical and emotional information. The amygdala region of the brain codes emotional memory with no reason or understanding. It processes emotions and feelings and does not record facts or data. It can attach emotion to neutral stimuli and is responsible for most of the behavioral conditioning and learning that have emotion in the brain.

In contrast, the hippocampus region of the brain codes logical and linear data without attaching feeling; it records facts and events. As stated by psychiatrist Dr. Glen Johnson: "We make meaning based on which part of the brain is activated, and we also go through cycles of right and left activation. If we are in a right-brained cycle when a trauma or event occurs, then we will make emotional meaning to the situation. If we are in a left-brained cycle, then we will make logical, unemotional meaning to the event as data."

Many factors contribute to why we make meaning out of our life experiences. Our tasks are to understand the working of our minds and to recognize our human tendencies. Then it is important to learn skills and to take action as we navigate through the maze of life.

Because of the amygdala, humans are meaning-making machines. For example, if your dad doesn't say he loves you when he ends a phone conversation, you may feel that you are not accepted, and you may attach a meaning that you are unlovable or worthless.

If you continue to look at things the same way, you will believe that this meaning is the only way to think about it. The exercises in this chapter will help you discover limiting beliefs and attached meanings.

Humans are meaning-making machines.

Beliefs can be either strengths or limitations. We are now searching for limiting beliefs that stop you from success. First, we will begin to recognize limiting beliefs, and then to discover the origin of your particular belief. I will then share with you some techniques to shift the beliefs into strengths.

Limiting beliefs can be changed!

The Sword in the Stone

Let's use the metaphor that a strong, firm belief is like a sword in a stone. The sword is stuck and immovable. While participating in the exercises below, notice how the sword will begin to just wiggle a little and loosen up a bit; and sometimes the sword will completely come out as you wonder how in the heck it was so stuck.

For the following examples, I am going to list some personal and professional beliefs. Keep in mind the personal and professional goals that you set, earlier, as we continue to find your self-sabotage. Look at the pyramid and identify how you process at each layer from the Environment to Actions, Skills, Beliefs & Values, Identity, and Purpose/Mission.

The following lists are examples of limiting beliefs. Notice the annoyances of the environment and what limiting beliefs you have about the actions you take and the skills you have developed. How do your beliefs affect you?

Limiting beliefs are in the categories of beliefs about your self, beliefs about others and beliefs about the world in general.

Environment

Personal Examples. I believe that:

- This suit looks bad on me.
- Blue is not my color.
- Being short is bad.
- I am out of control outside my environment.
- This city is too big for me.
- I dress too sexy at work.
- Some people are naturally thin.
- Everyone has a better voice than me.
- There are too many people in this city.

Professional Examples. I believe that:

- I am surrounded by chaos.
- I can't make money in this state.
- I can work best when I live on the East Coast.
- Money is hard to make in this industry.
- My cubicle is too small.
- My coworkers talk too much.
- Others were given money from their daddies.
- They are plain lucky to have what they have.
- They were in the right place at the right time.

List the limiting beliefs that you have noticed regarding the environment.

_____
_____
_____
_____

Actions

Personal Examples. I believe that:

- I talk too much.
- I don't talk enough.
- Playing golf too much is bad.
- I don't work out enough.
- I do too much.
- I need to serve more.
- I talk on the phone too much.
- Others judge.
- Others act rude.

Professional Examples. I believe that:

- You have to work 24 hours a day to be successful.
- No matter what I do I will fail.
- Filing is not important.
- I will never be good at accounting.
- Others work harder and make more money.
- Others are sharks in business.
- Others have more opportunity.
- Other people are lucky.

List the limiting beliefs you have noticed regarding Actions.

_____

_____

_____

_____

Skills

Personal Examples. I believe that:

- I can't think quickly.
- I've never been good at detail.
- I can't do it.
- I don't have enough patience.
- I can't remember things very well.
- Others will never be there for me.
- Others are better than me.
- Others are smarter than me.
- Other people have more talent.

Professional Examples. I believe that:

- I can't make money.
- I don't know how to sell.
- I can't manage my team.
- I don't have talent.
- I am not able to read my clients very well.
- I am not good at balancing my bank statements.
- Others are smarter at business.
- Other people just "get" how to run a business.
- Successful business owners are just sharks.

List the limiting beliefs you have noticed regarding Skills.

_____
_____
_____
_____

Beliefs/Values

Personal Examples. I believe that:

- I think negative thoughts too much.
- I act pessimistically.
- I can't control my beliefs.
- I value the wrong things.
- I will always be fat.
- I will eventually have my grandmother's body.
- I have a bad singing voice.
- Others think they are better than me.
- Others are lucky.

Professional Examples. I believe that:

- I am bad at sales
- I can't make a lot of money.
- I could never own my own business.
- I don't know what to say to my clients.
- I don't know my target demographic.
- I will never be able to prospect.
- Others believe that they are hot stuff because they have money.
- Others believe business is just easy.

List the limiting beliefs you have noticed regarding Beliefs.

_____
_____
_____
_____

Identity

There is a difference between the magnitude of a belief that is simply about the environment in contrast to a belief at the level of "I am." Notice that the beliefs at an "I am" level are beliefs about your core – who you are without a body. They are coded more deeply in the neurology and are used as nouns describing yourself.

Personal Examples. I believe that:

- I am ugly.
- I am a bad person.
- I am worthless.
- I am nothing.
- I don't deserve to be happy.
- I am less important than others.

Professional Examples. I believe that:

- I am not worthy of success.
- I am not worthy of being part owner of the company.
- I am not the kind of person who can have wealth.
- I am not good enough to be someone's boss.
- I don't know who I would be if I had money.
- I can't imagine what I would be like if I were successful.

List the limiting beliefs you have noticed regarding Identity.

_____

_____

_____

_____

Are you filling in all the answers, or browsing this section to use as a reference quide? Either way, there is a lot of information here, and you will want to revisit this section often. Notice which category of limiting beliefs you typically use. Start to recognize your patterns.

All beliefs that are not about **self or others** are grouped together in the World Beliefs category. Beliefs can be positive beliefs or limiting beliefs.

World Beliefs

Personal Examples. I believe that:

- The world is out to get me.
- The world is scary.
- We shouldn't make furniture out of trees.
- Technology is moving too rapidly.
- This life has only limited opportunity.
- There is no hope in the world.
- The world is evil.
- Life is too hard.

Professional Examples. I believe that:

- There is just no money with my name on it.
- Money doesn't grow on trees.
- The economy will fail before I have a chance to succeed.
- The world controls my abilities in business.
- Others hurt others.
- The economy is why I haven't succeeded.
- It is too late for me to jump on the train of success.
- It is hard to make money today.

List the World Beliefs you have discovered that may stop your success.

_____

_____

_____

_____

   In the next chapter we will go through a series of belief-shifting exercises. Your limiting beliefs may shift dramatically on the first exercise. If your beliefs shift, great; then pick another limiting belief and go through the exercises again. Perhaps you may want to see what would happen when you take one limiting belief through all the exercises.

   Anna was very ready to move on and looked like she just left the starting blocks of a 100-meter sprint. Anna took notes to categorize all the beliefs above, and she was learning how it all fit in the pyramid. She was beginning to understanding the levels of the pyramid and had already experienced some awakening moments.

Chapter Twelve:

OH, THE FABLES WE WRITE

How to be the author of your own fables and stories.

A t this point we are still on the Belief/Value level of the pyramid. Let's acknowledge that the beliefs you have are really stories or fables you have written.

Look at the list of limiting beliefs you wrote on the previous pages and say, "I have written a fable that ..." For example: "I have written a story or fable that I am unlovable." Go down your entire list. Before each limiting belief, say, "I have written a fable that…"

How does saying this shift your belief? Does the metaphorical sword in the stone begin to move a bit? Notice small or large shifts. What is it like to think of the belief differently now?

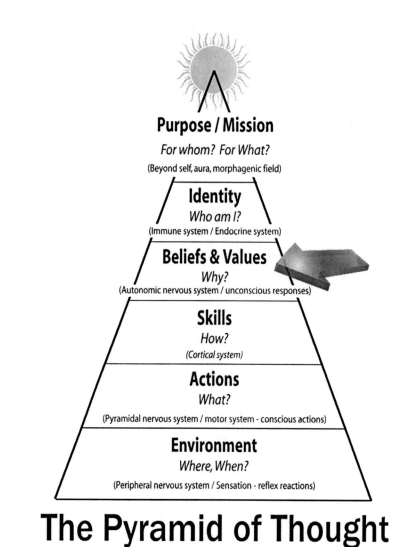

The Pyramid of Thought

When we change the way we are internally seeing or hearing, we will feel different.

Beliefs are one way of looking at things. If I look at a piece of paper straight on, it appears to be a white rectangle. Now I am quite certain that it is a white rectangle, and I would argue that point. I would stake my life on it and never change my mind. What if someone else looks at the paper from the side and sees a long, white, thin line? That person is looking at the same item, yet he or she is sure of seeing a line and not a rectangle. The two of us could debate forever and ever about our differing viewpoints. Only when we are willing to look at the paper from a different angle or point of view do we see a new perspective. Both parties are right about their own outlooks from their own specific perspectives.

A belief = One way of looking at something.

Keep in mind for the sake of jargon that:

Beliefs = Stories = Fables.

They are all the same, and I use the words interchangeably. Use the word that works best for you.

Belief Exercises Section

Analyze Your Beliefs Exercise:

Review the beliefs you listed earlier in the book. Which belief would you like to shift? Pick one limiting belief that you know is stopping you from either personal or professional success. Please fill in the spaces below. (Anna's responses appear in parentheses.) Anna chose the belief that her whole family was fat, so that was why she was fat.

1. **My limiting belief is:** (I'm doomed to be fat.)

_____

_____

_____

_____

2. **My limiting belief equation and attached meaning are:** (My family is fat = I will be fat.)

_____

_____

_____

_____

3. **Now pick what you would rather believe. I would rather believe:** (I can be thin.)

_____

_____

_____

_____

4. When did you first start to believe this limiting belief? Do you know? Are you aware? Do you have an idea or a sense? (My mom always used to blame her overweight mom for her own weight problem.)

_____

_____

_____

_____

5. Desired new belief: (I can be thin regardless of my heredity.)

_____

_____

_____

_____

6. See your new belief in your mind's eye. What does it look like? See yourself living in this new way. Then feel what it would be like to have this new belief.

_____

_____

_____

_____

Anna grinned from ear to ear. "You mean I am not doomed to be fat? Hey, I look good in my mind!"

She begged me to go on.

7. What is your new belief?

_____

_____

_____

_____

If your belief has shifted, then pick another belief to use for the next exercises. If not then use the same limiting belief in all the exercises until you have changed the belief.

Meaning Machine Exercise:

Since humans are so good at making meaning to things, we must also be able to shift the meanings.

- Think of a scenario where you made a meaning that is bothersome to you.
- Look at this situation from the side or from someone else's point of view.

1. What are four other meanings you could have made?

_____

_____

_____

_____

2. How does this open your mind to other possible meanings?

_____

_____

_____

_____

3. What will you now make this scenario mean? More choices?

_____

_____

_____

_____

Sorting Exercise:

Since our conscious minds can hold only a limited amount of information and stimulus at one time, our minds cope by something we call selective attention. We naturally select what we focus our attention toward. Try this. Look around the room and notice all the green that you see. Take your time. Now, let that go. Shift your attention now to all the yellow in the room; notice that shades of yellow pop into your conscious attention. Now look for all the red. As you look for red, are you aware that your eyes are searching and seeing shades of red? Now be aware that as you sort for red, the green fades into the background and the red comes to the foreground.

Have you ever noticed that when you are looking for a certain kind of car to buy, you all of a sudden seem to see that type of car everywhere? If you are going to put up a fence, do you notice that many homes have the same fence? Again, what you look for, you will find.

It is interesting that as we look for something, we always find it. What we focus on, we find. So how can we apply this in our lives? Let's say that you love your significant other, yet there are things about him or her that you don't necessarily like. You may like her eyes, but you don't like the burly mole on her chin. So, based on the model of sorting, focus on the eyes and all the things you like, and the things you don't like will fade into the background. Turning the situation around, wouldn't you hope that your significant other would sort for all of your good qualities instead of focusing on what he or she doesn't like about you?

Have you ever noticed that when you are looking for a certain kind of car to buy, you all of a sudden seem to see that type of car everywhere?

If you believe that people are rude, then sure enough, you will find rude people. If you believe that you are not lovable, you certainly will find people who don't love you, or you will notice others' unlovable actions and make them bigger than they are. These are examples of why a belief that is formed long ago becomes bigger and deeper each year.

Watch out what you are sorting for, because ... what you sort for, you will find.

"Anna, before we get busy with some visualization-belief-shifting exercises, I'd like to have you practice being aware of your internal visual pictures."

Anna was ready.

I had her visualize an apple. I had her see it on the floor in the middle of the room. I asked her how clearly she could see it on a scale from 1 to 10. What color of apple was she visualizing? She had a Gala red apple, she could see it about a 9, and she could even imagine smelling it. I had her move it up in the air 5 feet, move it to the right 3 feet or so, and then see it on my desk. "Now, Anna, if I were to ask you where you see the apple in your mind's eye, you would say on the desk. The apple is not really on the desk but in your mind's eye. It is not on the floor; it is on the desk, right?"

Anna thought that was cool. I had her imagine her dogs, parents, friends, and other things in her mind. She was becoming more aware of where in psycho-space she was seeing her internal pictures. I told her that this skill takes practice and is **so** powerful in helping her control her thoughts. My dad always said that you can't solve a problem until you know what the problem is. When you have a limiting feeling, your mind will **always** code it in a picture and in space. Your task is to become aware of what and where you see things. Then you will be prepared to **change limiting beliefs forever** with the following exercises.

If you want
CONTROL OF YOUR THOUGHTS,
Become VERY aware of
WHAT you are seeing and
WHERE you are internally seeing things.

Please practice and practice noticing your internal visual pictures. Then you can get busy changing your life for the better and experience living your dreams.

How are you doing with your notebook? Are you answering the appropriate questions and learning a lot about yourself? For the following exercises, you may want to follow the steps without filling anything out so that you can just experience the steps. It is up to you.

Psycho-Space Exercise:

One way to change a fable is to see it differently in your mind.

1. See the limiting belief or feel it.
2. Where in space do you see it or feel it? Is it directly in front of you? To your right? Out by the freeway? Do you feel it behind you or possibly in your body somewhere?
3. Now that you are aware of the space the belief seems to occupy, move it 2 feet to the right or left.
4. Change the location of the belief until you feel different.
5. How do you feel different?
6. What is your new belief?

Modeling-Contrast Exercise:

1. Look at the limiting beliefs you listed above.
2. Imagine that someone you respect and honor has this limiting belief.
3. Visualize this person that you respect, and plop the limiting belief on him or her. See this person act differently than he or she normally would. See how his or her demeanor, attitude, and actions change.
4. When you imagine the other person with the limiting beliefs, can you see how he or she would act differently? Is it more obvious now that it is only a belief and that beliefs are not real? Say you respect your neighbor. He is stalwart and positive. See him in your mind's eye with your limiting belief. How would he act differently?

5. What is your new belief?

Remember to differentiate between what is real and what is not real. If something is real, it can be proven scientifically, and the associated data is testable and tangible. If not, it is most likely a belief. If I believe I have offended you and I ask you if I have, and you say "yes," then the fact is that I offended you, and it is not a belief. Sometimes we need to check things out to see if they are real or if they are only beliefs.

I believe that my computer is evil, Anna said.

Hum, is that real or not real? Seems real…what if she shifted how she looked at her computer?

Anna said that her computer had a mind of its own and the only choice she had was to kill it.

I told her that there are many people that feel the same way and she would be able to use that limiting belief in the next few exercises.

Change Your Fable by Shifting the Picture Exercise:

Now, what happens when you realize that you are creating a wonderful fable? You are a creative writer and you write a fable that there are intimidating giants all around the town.

Example: Let's say my belief is that Jack is intimidating.

My equation is:

Jack is better than me = I am small and unimportant = I won't be able to give my speech with him in the room = I will fail = My dad will be disappointed in me = I am helpless = I may die.

I visualize how I see Jack. In my mind he is huge like a giant, probably 7 feet tall and 500 pounds. I see him in black and white, and my peripheral vision is narrow. I see only him and nothing else. He is moving slowly and the sound is muted. I hear a "Wah, wah," like the sound of an adult talking on the phone to Charlie Brown of *Peanuts*. I feel a pit in my stomach and a tension that makes me want to run. I am in trouble because running would just look wrong in front of all my colleagues, so instead I choke on my bile and smile a big one.

So what if I wrote a different fable? I begin to see Jack as actual size: 6 feet tall, 180 pounds. I see him breathing. I move this visual picture 2 feet to the right in my mind. I turn the sound dial in my mind, hear accurately, and maneuver the sound to come in both ears equally. I even play with making him smaller than life size – say 3 feet tall. I am having so much fun that I imagine that he takes his shirt off. I then wonder how I would feel if he had on a **pink tutu and tights.** Oh my! This is fun stuff.

I then quickly jerk my gaze to see what I really see in the room. Oh, I see my new cherry filing cabinet. Oh, I see the beautiful snow outside my window. Pause; breathe; now how do I feel about Jack? I now feel that Jack is just a person just like me trying to make a living, wanting to be liked by other people, and getting things done.

This technique is user friendly. When we change our unconscious representations, we can't feel the same. What fables do you need to rewrite?

Anna looked like a small child concentrating while putting little puzzle pieces in tiny, differently shaped compartments. She stared downward as her tongue poked out a bit in concentration. She insisted on going over and over her newfound beliefs with me. She wanted to practice shifting beliefs and rewriting fables. She was enamored by the Psycho-Space Exercise and the Meaning Machine Exercise.

I finally told Anna that we needed to stop blowing up and exploding all the people that she didn't like. I told her that the kids in the delinquent centers always used to get a kick at doing that visualization. They loved blowing up the guards in their minds and turning their heads around and around as in the movie *The Exorcist.* They enjoyed the lovely freedom they had in the privacy of their minds. I mentioned that we have options other than violence when we use this technique. Anna realized that she needed to settle down a bit and begin making more appropriate fables and visual pictures. I let her know we were not done, and there were more fun exercises to come.

Be careful what you visualize because that which you visualize, you will actualize.

"Well-Maybe" Exercise:

A question presupposes possibilities and opens up the sentence for discovery.

1. Write your limiting belief as a sentence: I believe that _____.
2. Put a **question mark** after your belief in place of the period.

    Examples:

    I am useless?
    I am unlovable?
    People always leave me?
    My dad doesn't love me?

3. How does that change the way you think about it? How does changing the period to a question mark dilute or dramatically alter your belief?
4. What is your new belief?

Rewrite Your Fables Exercise:

1. Write your limiting belief.
2. What is your limiting belief, and what is the attached meaning?
3. If you were able to see your limiting belief, what would it look like? Would it be in front of you or to your side? Is it in color or black and white?
4. Is it moving or still? Is your peripheral vision open or closed?
5. After you are aware of how you see your limiting belief in your mind's eye, change your visual representations. Start by moving the picture 2 feet to your right or left, and then breathe.
6. Change the color intensity either up or down.
7. Make the picture life size rather than larger or smaller than actual size.
8. Play with the picture and sound. Keep shifting and breathing until you feel different. Even small shifts will begin to make more sense throughout the day. All of a sudden you may say, "Hey, I feel different."
9. What is your new belief?

When you truly see the beliefs differently in your mind, you cannot feel the same. Understand that some people are not that great at being aware of their visual representations. If this is difficult for you, then I have more tricks in my bag besides changing visual representations. If you are great at visualization, then it will be a piece of cake.

Change Frame Exercise:

1. Write your limiting belief.
2. What is your limiting belief equation, and what is the attached meaning?
3. If you were to see your limiting belief with a frame around it, what color, size, and texture of frame would you see?
4. Now, change the frame's color and size. Breathe.
5. How is the belief different now?
6. What is your new belief?
7. How does changing this limiting belief assist you in reaching your goal?

Shifting a Feeling-Belief Exercise:

1. When you think of a limiting belief, what does your body feel?
2. Tap this part of your body and then tap all over your body for one minute.
3. Breathe hard in and out.
4. Move your eyes in a figure 8, eight times in both directions.
5. Jump up off the ground four times.
6. Get a drink of water.
7. How do you feel different?

Internal Eye Exercise:

This exercise works best for highly visually oriented people.

1. Look at your limiting belief or problem. Do you see it clearly and vividly?
2. As you become more aware of your internal representations, notice what happens when you cover up your right eye and look at your belief or problem. Remember to breathe.
3. After this feeling settles in, switch and cover your left eye. Pause, relax, and breathe. How do you view the situation differently? Covering your left eye in most cases causes you to think about your problem more logically instead of being emotionally invested.
4. What small or large shifts do you experience?

This exercise works best when you visualize the situation very clearly. The more sharply you can imagine seeing your problem, the better this exercise works. How does it work, you ask? Simply like this: When you cover the right eye, the left eye uses the right hemisphere of your brain where feelings and emotions are coded. Covering the left eye causes you to use your right eye, thus triggering access to the opposite hemisphere, the left. The left hemisphere is where you process logical, pragmatic, organized, and unemotional ways of thinking. This technique is very user friendly. If you are ever in a spot where you have too much emotion for your own good, cover your left eye and see the situation through your right eye.

Breathe and notice the emotional feelings shift to logic. When you want to have more emotion, cover the right eye.

What is your new belief?

_____
_____
_____
_____

_____

Hint:
Cover the LEFT eye to trigger
Logic and decrease emotion.
Cover the RIGHT eye to trigger
Emotions and feelings.

Shifting a Voice Exercise:

When you hear a voice that causes a limiting belief, do the following:

1. Identify whose voice it is.
2. Where is the voice? Is it behind you, in front, or to one side?
3. Grab the voice and hold it in your hand in front of you.
4. What do you want to keep about this voice? Own what you need to own.
5. Now blow the voice off your hand and let it go back to the person who sent it, or send it out to the sunset.
6. How do you feel different?

Anna finally began to slump on the couch. She had had it for the day and needed to rest, to let it all soak in. She was actually quite white as the color had faded from her skin. We decided to call it a day and meet next week. I explained that all this learning on deeper levels gets you tired. Again I explained that she needed to drink a lot of water and get plenty of rest. She was all for the resting part and went home to contemplate.

As Anna was leaving, I said, "Anna, when you come back for your next session, I will tell you a story about my dogs." She tilted her head in question and said, "OK, I will be ready."

Other Tools

Dogs are a man's best friend.

Another way to understand beliefs and meanings is to model someone or something that has what you want. Have you ever thought of modeling your dog? Now here is something really cool. We have two dogs, a Cocker Spaniel and a Maltese. When  we go on vacation, we take the dogs, of course. Beau is the Maltese, and he is really just like a 4-pound mouse with long white hair. He is a wimp, and I like to take him in my little doggy purse wherever we go. Lacey is a bigger dog, very stalwart and hardy at about 25 pounds. Sometimes when we go, we take Beau and leave Lacey in the hotel or washroom in the condominiums. I started to feel bad about Lacey's abandoned feelings. I imagined that she felt sad because Beau got to go with us and she had to stay behind. Then it occurred to me that Lacey was actually dumb and she didn't understand. As I contemplated the situation more, I realized that maybe Lacey was actually smart because she didn't attach the meaning of feeling bad that Beau got to go and she didn't. The actual meaning she makes is: "I am alone in the washroom." Period!

Here is another example. Beau can't eat table food because he will just throw it up. So when we give table food to Lacey and not Beau, what meaning does Beau make? Simply: "I want food and I'm not getting any."

Contrary to human beliefs, he is not making it mean that we like Lacey better.

We humanize our dogs and imagine that they think as humans do. They don't. They are only classically conditioned to paired stimuli. They connect two things together – for example, "sit" with "get a treat" or "come here and get petted." They pair the two activities without attaching any meaning. When they poop, they get put outside. Soon they are trained to choose their behaviors with the attached outcome. This is why dogs always forgive so easily and love unconditionally. They are 100 percent in the present moment. They don't create any meanings to situations. Wow, the lesson here is to act like your dog. Don't you wish your significant other acted more like a dog sometimes?

Pause Button

Since we are not dogs, we need to use creative strategies to begin to think more like them. I have something for you – a remote control. Imagine it is on the chair next to you. Go ahead and imagine you are picking it up. OK, there are a lot of really cool buttons on this remote. I want to introduce you to the <pause button>. When some scenario occurs and you begin to make a limiting belief or meaning, push the <pause button>.

For example, your friend is late for lunch, and you are at the restaurant waiting for her or him. Here are many possible stories that you could write. You begin to make fables or meaning that he or she:

- Is ditching you.
- Doesn't really like you.
- Doesn't respect your time.
- Forgot because he or she is dumb.
- Got in an accident and is dead.
- Is late because he or she can't find the restaurant.
- Planned for a different day and you miscommunicated.

Gee, which meaning should you use? How about none of them? Push your <pause button> and go into the nothing or neutral mode. Make no meaning yet. Wait to see. Clear your mind. Be open for possibilities. When your friend comes, then you will know the real meaning and realize you didn't need to waste your precious time writing fables.

My clients report that they use their <pause buttons> all the time! They come in so handy because they are so quick and effective. When you begin to use your <pause button> often, you will start to realize that beliefs or meanings are very subjective and not real.

Good job! Keep this book close by you and refer to the different exercises often. At some point you will have more understanding, and thus you will be able to control your thinking patterns. You will recognize sabotage quickly and notice thoughts that limit your success in your personal life and in your professional life.

Anna and I practiced. We took a few of her limiting beliefs and noticed the equations and fables that she had created. We changed internal pictures and sounds and used the change frame, the Psycho-Space

Exercise, and the <pause button> exercises. Her limiting beliefs were changing all over the place, and she was excited.

As she left my office, she was greeted by a frosty blizzard. She kicked a mound of translucent flakes and with a sincere giggle, she yelled, "Watch out, world, here I come!" Her silhouette disappeared into the blanket of white, and I knew she was learning to implement what it took to forge through the storm.

Now you can use these techniques to shift your limiting beliefs. You may find that you prefer one technique over another. It is interesting to play around with all of them.

Values

Values are items, activities, or people that are important to us at a core level. Our core purpose will manifest in our actions, beliefs, and feelings. Our values are unconsciously placed in a hierarchy within our minds. At times we may be confused about what is most important to us, really. We may forget what is of true value to us because of pressure from others and their opinions about job decisions, financial pressures, etc. We have many influences from family, friends, and even the media. When we know which values are most precious and sacred to us, we can more clearly make wise decisions and take more appropriate actions.

Rate Your Values Exercise:

List the top 15 things that are important to you – that you like or that you love – for example, family, associations, job, religion, health, freedom, dancing, etc.

1. _____
2. _____
3. _____
4. _____
5. _____
6. _____
7. _____
8. _____
9. _____
10. _____
11. _____
12. _____
13. _____
14. _____
15. _____

Now put a check mark by the five things you value most, if you had to give up the others completely to have the ones you have chosen.

Now, choose the top three and put a star by them.

Now choose one thing and circle it. Remember that you may have this one value only by giving up the others completely.

Hard to choose, eh? I think so. Yet now you know what you value most. My educated guess is that you would actually give up your life and die for this one thing you value most. Am I right? This value is at your core. Everything you do and pursue will support this one value. When you think of an item that you value, you will feel a deep spiritual and eternal connection. Keep this understanding close to your heart as you live your life to support that which you value most.

Review:

Let's review the rules we discussed in the beginning of this book. When learning a new skill or implementing a new way of thinking or being, it is vital to apply these important rules:

1. Be open and willing to take a look inside and change.
2. Never miss an appointment except for an emergency that involves blood or smoke.
3. Be willing to complete all assignments and tasks each week.
4. Read other books and pamphlets that I recommend to enhance and complement what I have taught you.
5. Teach what you have learned to someone else along the way. Deep and lasting change occurs when you teach concepts and principles to someone else.

Now assess where you are at this point. Answer yes or no, or fill in the blanks.

1. I have been open to what I can learn and change about myself. Y/N _____

2. I kept all appointments, and I have called two days ahead for needed schedule changes. (I have been consistent in following along in this book.)
Y/N _____

3. I have shared my learning's with someone else, and I have synergized my thoughts with him or her. Explain.

_____

_____

_____

_____

4. I have completed all the assignments and exercises that apply to me. Y/N _____

5. I have read some of the recommended books.
Y/N _____

6. What have I learned that I can apply in my personal life?

_____

_____

_____

_____

7. What have I learned that I can apply in my professional life?

_____

_____

_____

_____

8. I am willing to continue to complete assignments.
Y/N _____

9. I visualize the pyramid in my mind, and I will refer to it often as I walk through life. Y/N _____

You have learned many things that have possibly stopped you from success. You have discovered what may stop you in the environment, actions that may stop you, skills and abilities that you need to practice, beliefs that are limiting, and values that you hold dear. Using this knowledge base that you have developed, we will now transition into the area of inner-child work and identity development.

Anna reported that her favorite technique was the <pause button>. She used it daily and thanked me for inventing it. I told her that I hadn't invented it; I had just reminded her of what she already knew. "Anna, you had all the resources you needed before we met. I am just a reminder of the recipe and a third-party perspective as your coach."

This week Anna had discovered many limiting beliefs. After she ran them through the exercises, one at a time, we came to the space where she had no limiting beliefs about being thin and making calls comfortably each day. She was elated and had already lost more than 10 pounds. She had closed more deals in the last month than she had closed in the last year.

Her relationships with coworkers, men, and her family of origin were becoming more enhanced each day. She had even gone skiing with a group of friends, and they had decided to make it a weekly excursion. Her skin shone from a newly acquired tan. She had a bit of a raccoon look from her snow goggles. Life for Anna was looking up.

Please consider what changes you will make **both personally and professionally.**

What actions will you take?

_____
_____
_____
_____

What skills have you developed or need to develop?

_____
_____
_____
_____

What mental processes/beliefs and values, have you discovered and shifted?

_____
_____
_____
_____

Chapter Thirteen:

SELF-ESTEEM
FOR THE SUMMIT
Find Out Who You Really Are
Deep Down Inside

As much as I love meeting with clients each day, frankly, there are times when the need envelops me to sun-drench my body in a warm, aesthetic atmosphere. I told Anna that I would return in about a week.

I find myself five hours south of my mountain home, overlooking a small, bubbly, man-made river against the red rocks of southern Utah. The golf course is a green oasis backed by the magnificent jagged rocks of Snow Canyon.

The ability to contemplate and appreciate God's creations overtakes my breath and stimulates my abilities to take in color, air, and peace. I notice that God's nature claims peace, and His plans are not in conflict. The red flowers bask by the yellow flowers, and next to the rough textures of rock and gravel I see silky soft leaves. God's nature is always in balance like a melodic symphony. As erosion occurs, valleys are created and great lakes are changed. Earth's natural state is harmonious, and I yearn to mind-meld with the energy I feel from the scenery. The diversity of all that occurs is congruently manifesting a peaceful environment for me to relish.

My mind goes to **The Nothing.** Have you ever experienced The Nothing? The body feels heavy and the mind is light. Colors swirl in a symmetrical direction, cleansing all that is not needed. The Nothing begins to create a space for further questions, deeper needs for understanding, and greater acknowledgment of unanswered whys.

*Have you ever experienced
The Nothing?*

As I return to my conscious awareness, slowly I awake to ponder the reason I am alive and why I exist. Who am I and who are you? Who are we really? Why do we breathe and why do we live? What is the purpose of all life? In particular, what is the purpose of my life? Questions about my identity and purpose encircle me.

Then it comes as though God is speaking to me, directly in my heart and mind. This life is about love. This life is about understanding how to navigate through its obstacles with our physical bodies and how to overcome our weaknesses. *This life is about progress and refinement of our souls that have existed before this life as intelligence and that will exist throughout all eternity.* Love is the center of the light of the universe, and love is the controlling force that causes the flowers to bloom and the water to flow. We are loving beings, and we have forgotten this fact because of the metaphoric shield placed between the memories of this life and our existence before birth. I wonder to myself how this knowledge will help Anna. How will this knowledge help you? How do you think about your activities today when considering the truth that life is about love?

Life is about love.

I find myself sitting in a pool of energetic light. My respect and honor for all living things is nourished and increasing. I think of you, my reader. Do you know who you are? Do you know who you are without a body? Do you know your purpose? If you knew the answers to these questions, would you live with more passion and reason?

Has your passion ever created in you an insatiable thirst for knowledge? Has this passion ever led you to enthusiastically research a subject at a library? Have you ever earnestly researched a topic on the Web? Did you ever dissect a frog in seventh grade and learn what was really inside its fat belly? Have you ever wondered what it would be like to look inside your soul and see what is really there?

Has your view of yourself been altered by what others think, leading you to see yourself through a dark colored glass? Would you like to shake off caring what others think about you? Would you like to liberate your mind of thoughts that cause paralysis, fear of the future, and many other problems?

I know that as you progress through this chapter and learn who you are and who you were before this earthly life, you will discover that you are a beautiful person. As you learn more about who you are deep down (your soul), and about how you esteem yourself (your identity), you will experience changes that will help you stop stopping yourself. You will find that you are full of light and purpose. You are important no matter what you have done in your life up to this point. You are magnificent.
This I know!

You are magnificent!

I returned from my southern Utah sanctuary anxious to meet with Anna to learn how she was applying her new beliefs.

When Anna and I met, she eagerly shared many "Aha!" moments that she had experienced. Although she had completed her assignments, she still felt she had hit a wall that prevented her from understanding her inner core and her higher purpose. As we talked, Anna noticed the pain in her stomach return – that same dramatic pain she felt during our first session. I commended her for her awareness. I reminded her that the stomach was receiving communications from the unconscious, and that we would address this situation soon. I briefly considered some strategies involving identity that we could use that would shed light on the meaning of these pains and that would be helpful in resolving them. Pains like Anna's are a common occurrence and a topic that we will visit in chapter 14.

Many say, "I want to find out who I am." What if we stated this differently and said, "I want to find out who I was"? Several founders of psychology have concluded that we are indeed perfect and beautiful at our beginnings. Infants are good and pure, and so is the essence of each person's being. Life experiences have covered us with limiting beliefs and fables. To find our true inner selves, we need to clearly understand who we were before we formed limiting beliefs. When we can clearly separate who we really are from what we do, we are able to find great self-esteem based on our insides instead of our outsides. Sometimes our interpretation of societal expectations causes us to combine our actions with who we think we are (our identity).

As we review the pyramid, notice the Identity level near the top. The Identity level is wired deep inside you. Your identity is who you think you are at a core level but your soul/spirit is who you really are, who you are deep down inside. It always has been and always will be the same. It never changes; it only becomes suppressed and forgotten.

So far we have focused on understanding parts, beliefs, and values. Now we probe deeper into the beautiful inner self, the unconscious, the inner child. If your sabotage is hidden at the Identity level, we will respectfully discover where the problem lies. If you are stopped at this level, be patient with yourself as you learn why you are stopped and what to do about it.

Your identity is what you think about who you are, deep down, at a core level.

Your core is your soul/spirit. Your soul existed before you were born.

What you think about who you are, if negative, is the problem.

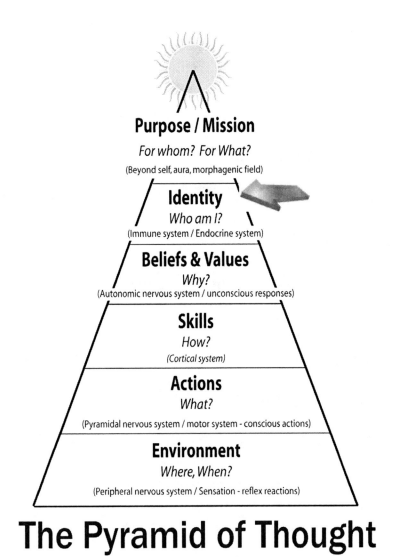

Purpose / Mission
For whom? For What?
(Beyond self, aura, morphagenic field)

Identity
Who am I?
(Immune system / Endocrine system)

Beliefs & Values
Why?
(Autonomic nervous system / unconscious responses)

Skills
How?
(Cortical system)

Actions
What?
(Pyramidal nervous system / motor system - conscious actions)

Environment
Where, When?
(Peripheral nervous system / Sensation - reflex reactions)

The Pyramid of Thought

"How do I know I am stopped at this level?" you may wonder. Ask yourself this question: "Do I deserve the goal that I set at the first of this book?" If the answer is "no," then you are stuck at this level. Now consider other goals and ask these questions. Do you deserve success? Do you deserve to have good things? Do you deserve to be loved? Can you clearly answer the question, "Who am I?" Can you describe who you would be if you were just a soul or spirit without a body? If "yes," great! If not, you are stuck at this level.

It is even more applicable at the Identity level to understand as we probe more deeply inside our feelings and emotions, that the English language falls terribly short.

What stops you from achieving your goal on the Identity level?

Personal:

(Anna said that she was stopped at the Identity level because she didn't feel that she deserved to be fit and beautiful. She couldn't imagine who she would **be** if she was smaller.)

Reader's response:

_____
_____
_____
_____

Professional:

(Anna was confusing who she really is—her soul, with her identity; who she thinks she is. Her identity was connected to struggling and fighting for money. She couldn't imagine who she would **be** if she were in control of her financial life.)

Reader's response:

_____

_____

_____

_____

Read on, to learn how each category is unique.

1. I Do: (Verbs) *Actions* level on the pyramid. Actions are something that somebody does.

Examples: I Do (verbs):

- I dance.
- I move my arm.
- I sing.
- I do accounting.
- I sell financial services.
- I paint.
- I pet my dog.

2. Characteristics: (Descriptions, no particular place on the pyramid.) Characteristics are qualities that you develop by acting a certain way over and over.

Examples: Characteristics (I have):

- I have integrity, faith, and charity.
- I have confidence, passion, and honesty.
- I have respect, conscience, and courage.

3. I Am: (Nouns) *Identity* level on the pyramid. Describing who you really are deep down inside, independent of actions.

Examples: I Am (nouns):

- I am passion.
- I am love.
- I am progress.
- I am honesty.
- I am creativity.
- I am discovery.
- I am wisdom.
- I am light.

Do you notice the difference in feeling, between the "I AM" words and the "I DO" words? If not, take your time to feel. Notice on the pyramid, how far apart the Actions level is from the Identity level.

The Character descriptions ought to **feel** as though they are half-way between the "I Do" and "I AM" list. After some practice you will get better at recognizing the difference in feeling between the three categories.

I Do/I Am Exercise:

The following exercise will assist you in finding the real inner you.

1. Create your three lists on the next page. (Most people have a much bigger "I DO," list than "I AM," list. "I AM" descriptions have so much meaning in each word. My clients usually come up with about five to eight profound "I AM" words/statements.) After filling out the table, come back to this section and move to step 2.

Hint:

To find your "I Am" statements, it is helpful to  *remember what you were like at age 5, when you were at your emotional prime and before life began to take a toll.*
(Did you experience any abuse at age 5? If you did, just focus on the questions above rather than thinking about when you were 5 years old.)

---

2. Check your "I AM" words/statements, using the **"Checking your I AM's"** located after the table.
3. Choose one "I AM" statement that is not a current strength – one that you have not successfully performed lately. Practice this quality every day and turn it into a strength. **Write it in your planner** to

remind yourself to focus on this quality every day for one week. Apply this quality as often as possible and next week, choose another "I AM" statement to practice.

4. Be sure to clearly separate what you do from who you are! You are **not** what you do.

Please fill out the following table:

I Do (verbs)	Characteristics	I Am (nouns)

After you have filled out the table, go over each "I AM" word/statement, with the following questions:

Checking your "I AM 's"

1. Finish this sentence: "I am _____."
2. Can you **be** this quality without having a body? Y/N _____. (A true "I AM" statement answers "yes" to this question.)
3. Can you **be** this quality without doing anything? (A true "I Am" statement answers "yes" to this question.)
4. If you took the quality away, would your soul cease to exist? (The answer needs to be "yes." If the answer is "no," then your statement is not a true "I AM" statement.)

Now go back to the steps in the "I Do, I AM" Exercise, on pages 157, 158 and follow the instructions.

Here is a great example of how to separate what you **do** from who you **are** and how it assists in positive self esteem:

Some Indian tribes introduce themselves like this: **"Hi, I am known as Running Deer."** Notice they do not say, **"I am** Running Deer"; rather, they say, "I am known as Running Deer." If you say, "Hi, **I am** a doctor," I may reply, **"No, you aren't;** you work as a doctor." This really shows how we can stay in touch with our core being and disconnect ourselves from titles and labels. Instead, you can say, "I work as an architect," or "I work as a therapist," or "I work as a builder." In the future, notice how many times you slip and say, for example, **"I am** fat," or **"I am** tired," or **"I am** dumb." **Shift your words to say,** "My body has

155

too much fat on it," or "I feel tired right now," or "I acted dumb." By shifting your words, you will begin to clearly separate who you are from what you do.

One of my greatest pet peeves is when attendees of addiction recovery programs stand up at their meetings and say, "Hi, my name is _____, and **I am** an alcoholic." I recommend my clients say, "Hi, my name is _____, and I make high-risk drinking choices, and **I am** a child of God."

The unconscious mind is not smart enough to know that you didn't mean what you said, so it takes your words literally. It believes everything you tell it; **we must choose our words wisely.**

Be aware that identity development is a very powerful state of fulfillment. Identity is important, yet the Identity level on the pyramid is equal in importance to the other levels. Not one of the pyramid levels outweighs the others in importance.

The relationship between who you are deep inside and your actions is strong and can be confusing. Understanding two main ideas will help clarify this relationship. First, who you are is separate from what you do. For example, you have worth as a child of God despite your actions that may make you feel worthless. If your sense of worth depends only on your actions or anything else that is temporary, then you will feel worthless if and when things change. If it is based on who you are deep inside, you will always feel worthwhile. The second concept is that certain actions you take can eventually affect your identity. The essence of who you are will not change. Yet, you can cover up this essence and make yourself very uncomfortable in the process. For example, Natalie is honesty. This is her identity. When she acts dishonestly, she suffers because her true inner-self is not being expressed and she is out of harmony with her essence. Our actions ought to compliment and express who we are. When they do not, we feel pain.

Our actions ought to compliment who we are, deep inside.

I had a wonderful "Aha!" moment while watching one of the Batman movies on the big screen. One of the main characters in the movie kept saying to Batman, "Remember, **It is not who you are deep inside that matters; it's your actions that define you.**"

Since this theme is the opposite of what I teach, I tilted my head, scratched my chin, and squinted my eyes in thought, in an attempt to understand the intent of this statement. As the Bible says, our actions are the fruit of our labors, and our actions and who we have become inside our hearts are ultimately what God will judge us by. In my opinion, we won't go to heaven for our intentions, but rather for our actions and what's in our heart, such as love, honor, and caring.

I had a client a few years ago who worked intently on building his self-esteem and internal identity. After his long journey of discovery, he could finally utter the words, "I am great, I honestly love myself, and I love who I am." This profound declaration of inner progress and sense of light filled his soul. For the first time he felt peace. Well, after a few months I got a call from his ex-wife. On the other end of the line, I heard her pain as she stated that he had not paid child support for a year, did not have a job, did not visit the children, did not return things he had borrowed, and many more complaints.

At his next session, I realized more than ever before that actions are **as** important as identity. All the love he could muster for himself fell short because of improper actions or lack of pertinent actions. Thus, we must acknowledge actions, skills, **and** mental processes to achieve healing and peace.

Separate who you are from what you do so that you are able to love yourself and see through the muck to who you really are. This vision can help you create behavior and characteristics that complement who you are deep inside. This is why the "I Am/I Do" exercise is important. Completing this exercise can help you develop characteristics that may not be part of who you really are, but are still helpful. By practicing the actions of your "I AM statements," it strengthens your soul and causes your identity to be in line with who you really are.

One of my clients, who we'll call Ryan, grew up like many people, believing that his actions determined his worth. If he got A's and did well at sports, he was the "Good Boy," in the eyes of teachers, parents and eventually in his own eyes. He was connecting his worth to his actions. If he got bad grades or made mistakes, he was the "Bad Boy." After trying the "I Am/I Do" Exercise, Ryan began to see that he was not his actions. One of his strong "I AM's" was: "I am Patience." He was out with his friends, eating pizza one night, and was really trying to live, feel and experience "I am Patience." He was getting dis-couraged thinking of all the things he could not do perfectly, including acting patient. It hit him that acting patiently may strengthen who he really is, "Patience." So he acted patiently throughout dinner by listening to his friends' stories and giving them a high five. Through practicing this exercise for a few weeks, he began to change. He said to me:

> "It became more clear in my mind that
> I AM Patience, even if I don't act patiently all
> the time. I have worth because of who I am, not
> what I do. My actions can be worked on. If I
> am trying to do my best, my worth is good on
> its own. If I do politics or sports well, that is
> great! If I fail, that is too bad and I am not
> shaken; my worth is still great because of who I
> am. When I make mistakes, I forgive myself,
> solve problems, learn new skills, and move on.
> I no longer base my worth on what I do."

Isn't this good stuff? I know it's helping your identity. I hope that you and Anna are learning to understand that you are special, unique and that there will never be anyone just like you. Independent of your actions you are distinctive and original. You have an important place and purpose!

God calls himself the "Great I AM!" He says over and over, "I AM that I AM." Is it starting to make sense why? He has a pure spirit and his identity and his actions are in perfect alignment with who he is.

After reviewing and practicing the exercise for a few weeks, Anna finally said, "I get it!"

Chapter Fourteen:

THE VIEW FROM THE TOP

*A New Perspective on Healing
the Inner Child*

C hildren have qualities that God has said we
need to exemplify to be able to progress and
go to heaven. These childlike qualities are a
reflection of pure love, innocence, and acceptance;
they are qualities to nurture and desire beyond all else.
Please do not confuse child<u>like</u> attributes with
child<u>ish</u> attributes or with the **unhealed child within.**

Childlike attributes are to be cherished.

List the current childlike attributes that are strengths in your life. Explain why they are strengths.

_____

_____

_____

_____

Dissociation and Association

Let's play hide and seek. Now I see me, now I don't.

"Anna," I said, "we are going to do some great childhood exercises and **before** we proceed, there is something you need to learn and understand. You need to clearly know when you are **dissociated** and when you are **associated**. **Dissociated** is when you are imagining you are **out** of your body looking at yourself. **Associated** is when you are **in** your body, from your perception. As you sit on that couch, **can you do that?**"

Dissociation: Being **out** of your body in your mind's eye and being able to see yourself from a distance.

Association: Being **in** your body looking through your eyes and feeling **your own** feelings. When you are associated, you can't see yourself.

Anna tried and **nope,** she couldn't do it. **She could not see herself in her mind's eye.**

I asked her to get up off the couch and sit in another chair across the room and imagine seeing herself, over there, sitting on the couch. She could get an idea of what she looked like but still could not see herself clearly. I handed her a mirror that I conveniently had by me. (Since it is common that my clients can't dissociate well, I have a mirror handy.) As I handed her the mirror, I asked her to look into it and study her face. I asked her to shut her eyes and notice if she could see her face in her mind's eye. She practiced about five times, and finally she was able to see her face with her eyes shut. Then I had her view her shoulders through the mirror, shut her eyes, and notice if she could see her shoulders in her mind's eye. Again she practiced about five times before seeing her shoulders. Then she continued down her body. She practiced seeing her hips and arms and knees and legs and feet through the mirror until she could see her entire body, in her mind's eye, sitting on the couch.

I asked her, "When we started this exercise, how well could you see yourself over there on the couch? On a scale of 1 to 10, 10 being the clearest?" She said about a 1. As we continued to practice, she began to see herself, and she rated her ability about a 5. Soon she was an 8.

I gave her the assignment to stand in front of a full-length mirror when she got home and practice seeing herself in her mind's eye with her eyes shut. I told her to open and close her eyes while taking a look and then, with her eyes shut, to notice what she could visualize. I recommend that you do the same. You will soon be quite good at seeing yourself from a **dissociated** position. I told her to keep practicing until she could rate her ability to see herself from a dissociated position as a 9 or 10. I recommend that you, as my reader, do the same.

Some people see themselves too well and imagine seeing themselves constantly as though they have a little camera to the side, watching their every move. This causes people to be very critical of themselves and to be less present and less in touch with their real and accurate feelings. There is an appropriate time to be associated and an appropriate time to be dissociated. We will discuss these ideas in more detail.

"Now, Anna, let's practice **associating.**" I gave her an example. I told her a story of the time my grandpa was dying. He was a prominent man in the government, and as he aged, he began to lose his dignity. In the past several years, he had gone from a position in the White House Cabinet that brought him in contact with the President of the U.S., to sitting in a recliner chair in diapers. He was never a real "touchy-feely" person, and he had never told me that he loved me until he had only a few hours to live.

As I was telling the story to Anna, I talked with no emotion because I was **dissociated,** imagining I was out of my body, just off to the side of myself. When I associated into my body, with my eyes and heart centered, my eyes began to well up with emotion.

On his deathbed, my grandpa looked at me, and in a rattling voice, with tubes down his throat, he mustered the strength to say, "I love you, Darlene." Anna drank in my words. There was a moment of thick silence. My eyes began to moisten with tears of love for my grandpa and gratitude for his life. The thought of his passing lay heavily on my heart.

It was rewarding to see Anna practice and learn. She had empathy for me while I was telling my story, and her eyes even began to glisten as I expressed my feelings.

When I am **dissociated,** I can tell the story with no emotion, but when I am **associated** into the feelings, I am taken back in time; I can see his face and feel his warm hands in mine. I can barely talk.

Are you able to recognize when you are **associated** and **dissociated?** This technique comes in handy quite often, and it helps you to achieve an objective point of view. Now let's talk about the different positions. As you can see in the diagram, we all view the world from positions called **Self, Other, and Observer.**

Three Perspectives

1. "Self" is one's own perspective.

From this perspective, you are aware of your own feelings, perceptions, and thoughts. You realize they are your thoughts. You are in your body and can view the world with your own thoughts and feelings. **In the Self position, you are associated.** You feel emotions in the **Self** position. You may feel happiness, sadness, or other emotions.

2. "Other" is empathy – what you pick up that another may feel.

Empathy is the state of imagining you are someone else. You are **dissociated from yourself.** You begin to breathe like the other person and use his or her mannerisms. You can imagine feeling his or her feelings. The **Other** position is a place of empathy. When I was telling the story of my grandpa, Anna was in the **Other** position because she was feeling my feelings.

3. "Observer" is the perspective of a fly on the wall or an angel watching over things.

In this position, you are **dissociated. Observer** is a perceptual position as if you are a fly on the wall – looking at yourself, seeing your profile, and also looking at the other person you may be talking to. This position is objective and nonjudgmental. In **Observer** position, your perception needs to be about 5 feet away, not just out a little. You can see yourself AND the other person or persons. Move your perception so that you imagine being an **equal distance** between both you and the others. Notice the interaction between the person that looks like you, and the other person. When the person that looks like you, does something others react to it. When the others do something, you react. Notice the relationship dance.

This week, practice being aware of the three positions. Become aware of which perceptual position you are in the most. When do you tend to move in and out of each perception? Realize that **everyone** already moves among all three of the positions many times during each day. You are already doing it, but the goal is to diagnose and **control what position you are in.** It is recommended that a person spend most of his or her time in **Self** position and switch to **Other** and **Observer** and back many times a day. It is really important, from this moment forward, to be **aware** of which position you are in, so that we can continue discovering.

Many of my overweight clients are not able to see themselves accurately from a dissociated perspective. Many times just being able to see the reality of what they look like immediately causes them to begin to release weight.

Childhood Memories Exercise:

The following exercise will begin to uncover or shake loose some childhood memories. This is a great exercise to precede further work on the pyramid.

 Stand or sit in the corner of a room (by yourself, of course, or others may think you are really strange). Hold a pad of paper and pen in your hand. **Imagine and pretend that you are only one day old.** Can you do that? If you don't have memories, just pretend. Now write one sentence about what you remember or what you imagine might have happened when you were one day old. You may write something like: "There is family all around," or "I am alone. My mom is holding me. It is warm," or "I am cold." Understand that your unconscious mind – the part of your mind that never sleeps, the part of your mind that helps you not roll off your bed at night – remembers every detail of being one day old.

Now don't go away; stay with me. Yes, the unconscious does remember. If you don't consciously remember, that is really OK. Be open so you can feel, sense, and possibly, consciously remember.

Now, take a literal step, (or imagine stepping forward,) and pretend that you are one year old. Write a sentence that tells what you remember about being one. Now step forward into age 2 and write a sentence. Do this for every year until age 25. If you are older than 25, take a step for every 5 years of age, writing one sentence, until you have reached your current age.

IMPORTANT: If a memory is too painful, simply acknowledge it and step around it, and we will revisit it later. There is no purpose in triggering a painful experience for this exercise.

For this exercise, be as **associated** with your feelings as possible. Go back in time and remember being and feeling a certain age. **Get in your body**, and look through your eyes at the events and feelings you experience at that particular age. Then write the event and feelings using "I" instead of "she" or "he."

List a one-sentence memory for each of the following ages. Find any memory that comes to mind, be it positive or limiting. The purpose is to shake loose general memories of your past.

(To help memories surface, you can refer to school years rather than ages. If this is your preference, just write the school year by your age.)

Birth: _____

One day old: _____

Age 1: _____

Age 2: _____

Age 3: _____

Age 4: _____

Age 5: _____

Age 6: _____

Age 7: _____

Age 8: _____

Age 9: _____

Age 10: _____

Age 11: _____

Age 12: _____

Age 13: _____

Age 14: _____

Age 15: _____

Age 16: _____

Age 17: _____

Age 18: _____

Age 19: _____

Age 20: _____

Age 21: _____

Age 22: _____

Age 23: _____

Age 24: _____

Age 25: _____

Age 30: _____

Age 35: _____

Age 40: _____

Age 45: _____

Age 50: _____

Age 55: _____

Age 60: _____

Age 65: _____

Age 70: _____

Age 75: _____

Age 80: _____

Age 85: _____

Wasn't that an interesting trip through time? Now look at what you wrote. What patterns do you notice throughout your life? Are you commonly collecting things, being shy, loving others, being social or antisocial, etc.? List the patterns that you noticed in your past. At this point, don't decide if the pattern is good or bad. Just notice the patterns.

List the patterns that you noticed.

_____

_____

_____

_____

The Inner Child

It is interesting to understand how we develop as children. Each age experiences a different formation and developmental stage. When there is a bump in life or something stops you as a child from fully experiencing and developing in the appropriate manner, your beliefs are formed and your development is retarded or stopped. You then remain stopped or stagnated at that age. As you physically grow, there seems to be a split from the past-you and the present-you. Metaphorically, your inner child lives in you with wants and needs from the past that are not met in the present. The limiting beliefs formed during these bumpy times become frozen inside you. As you biologically age and have a like or similar bumpy experience, your limited beliefs intensify and become rooted even more deeply.

You and Anna are now becoming more aware of how past experiences affect you today. As I was explaining this idea to Anna, she said, "I can't believe this. I can't believe how truly simple it all is." I agreed with her and stated that things we understand are easy to achieve.

I continued explaining the stages of development to Anna. Psychoanalyst Erik Erikson, in his book *Identity and the Life Cycle,* maintains that there are eight stages of human development. He determined that personality injuries in childhood that are manifested in limitations can be traced to unresolved issues in specific stages of a person's life. Knowing at what stage your development was damaged can help you know where to focus your efforts to uncover and heal the past.

Erikson's Stages of Life

Erikson's stages are:

Ages 0–1:	Trust vs. Mistrust
Ages 2–3:	Autonomy vs. Shame
Ages 4–5:	Initiative vs. Guilt
Ages 6–11:	Industry vs. Inferiority
Ages 12–21:	Identity vs. Role Confusion
Ages 20–30:	Intimacy vs. Isolation
Ages 30–50:	Generativity vs. Stagnation
Age 55 and up:	Ego Integrity vs. Despair

As I meet with clients hour after hour and day after day, I notice patterns and similarities. I will be referring to Erikson's stages of life and expanding them. The ages listed below are based on my experiences and are, in my opinion, the most common ages for a person to develop limiting beliefs. Together, we search for interruptions or bumps in your road of life that caused emotional injuries.

Each stage has appropriate learnings and questions that are asked. If there is an emotional interruption at any stage, then limiting beliefs are formed and commonly carried throughout life. Listed below are the appropriate learnings of each age.

Newborn:

- Connection
- Vulnerability
- Vital need for attachment
- Need for constant nurturance with food, love, and physical care
- Ability to receive
- Development of security and safety

A person who has an interruption at this age may manifest, as an adult, an abnormal fear of abandonment and insecurity. He or she can be desperate to find someone to rely on for stability and security, and he or she may have a difficult time trusting others.

Ages 2–3:

- The child starts to become independent.
- The child begins to feel a sense of self, separate from the parent.
- The child learns to control the physical body.
- Identity is beginning to form.
- Selfishness is an important stage to help the child feel as though he is separate and not an extension of the parent.

A person who has an interruption at this age may manifest, as an adult, feelings of unworthiness, worthlessness, and being unlovable. Such people may develop a deep sense of shame, feeling that they are a mistake. They may justify their rights only by their importance to others, and they may apologize frequently and inappropriately. They may have a hard time saying "no" to others. They may avoid new experiences and fear others' anger.

Ages 4–5:

- Independence or being an individual becomes clearer.
- The realization of beginning to be separate from the parent heightens the child's sense of vulnerability.
- Trust and mistrust are at a more conscious level.
- The desire to please the parent starts to develop.
- The need to be recognized is forming.

A person who has an interruption at this age may manifest, as an adult, feelings of being afraid to make mistakes, helplessness and guilt, avoiding risks, and feeling unsafe. He or she may feel "not good enough." "Doing" and "being" get too closely connected, so the identity is contingent upon "doing" well rather than just "being" good. People who are interrupted at this age may become "people pleasers."

Ages 6–11:

- The ability to understand right from wrong is becoming complete. Moral development is forming. (Moral development involves more abstract thinking than just black and white or right and wrong.) The ability to understand morality and integrity begins to form.
- The ability to feel true empathy with understanding and possibly wisdom is forming.
- Protection of the self-identity and comparisons with others begin.
- Peer influence and experimentation are heightened.
- They are open to learning about others and realizing that there are more than just themselves in the world.

A person who has an interruption at this age may manifest, as an adult, feelings of being critical of himself or herself, avoiding all forms of competition, or being overly competitive to prove something. They may feel insecure and inferior. He or she may feel odd and unaccepted. He or she may try hard, in inappropriate ways, to prove he or she is OK.

Age 12:

- The start of puberty may cause feelings of being ungrounded, not safe, and powerless. Or the preteen adapts and is excited for the changes.
- The need for consistency in life circumstances and the need for foundation are important so that the teen can be free to discover and develop.
- Self-discovery is heightened.
- Self-doubt is common.

A person who has an interruption at this age may manifest, as an adult, feelings of being panicked to find themselves, looking to any relationship to help them be whole. They feel doubt in most areas, especially relationships with parents, siblings, and friends.

Age 16:

- A 16-year-old will not usually think or talk about the future, at least not out loud. Contemplation about the future is commonly suppressed yet occurring unconsciously.
- Teens at this age are more likely to live in the present and focus on the moment rather than the past or future.
- Pulling away from parents becomes necessary for the transition into adulthood.
- Identity development continues.

- Teens at this age will begin to wonder and discover as their identity is growing. One day they may be a Bowhead or a Punker or a Rocker. "Who am I?" they ask.
- Thrill seeking can be an expression of their personalities.

If parents use the strict authoritarian model, teens may foreclose or give up their identities and take on their parents' identities to please them or avoid confrontation. This may only backfire later in life and become a midlife crisis.

A person who has an interruption at this age may manifest, as an adult, a feeling of being incomplete, as though he or she missed out in life. He or she will wonder who he or she really is.

Age 18:

- Sexual connections develop.
- Stability is developed and completed.
- Thrill seeking may continue or decrease.
- Wondering about belonging to whom and to what is a vulnerable feeling at this age.
- Love for life and others is heightened.
- Passion and purpose are completing formation. (Feelings of passion and purpose during the course of life will stem from this developmental stage.)

A person who has an interruption at this age may manifest, as an adult, the need to look to external actions to feel accepted and acknowledged. He or she may have an insecure sense of self; doubt is common. He or she may not have a sense of purpose or passion.

There you have it. Most limiting beliefs in adulthood can be traced to the origin of an interruption in development during childhood. Interruptions before age 18 are coded more deeply than if they occur during adulthood. This is because, in childhood, cells are dividing and growing, and thus the limiting beliefs and feelings are growing along with the cell division. It is not to say that trauma can't happen later in life. It can. It may be possible to have a trauma imprint later in life, yet when it occurs, it is not as deeply wired and is much easier to resolve.

"Whoa, buddy," exclaimed Anna. "I think that I have tons of inner children deep inside of me that are starving and near death. I never thought of it that way. I just thought I was completely messed up. Will you give me some examples so I am clear about how the imprint, or whatever you call it, happens before age 18? It seems like I have had so much muck happen when I was older that it has ruined my life. I didn't realize that it had anything to do with my childhood."

I gave her this example: I have two different male clients about age 45. The wives of both men left them for other men. The first client was rejected constantly as a child. During his time with his wife, he felt stuck and hopeless for years. He would sort the world to feel rejected. He reported that his boss rejected him and his friends rejected him, and he even wondered if his dog wanted to be around him. Rejection was what he knew. He finally remarried and experienced intense jealousy issues because rejection was coded deeply inside him.

My second client had the same issues with his wife. During childhood, he had a stable family and never experienced rejection at any time that he could remember. He was well liked and received openly by the girls and his peers. When his wife first left him, he was definitely traumatized. He lost about 50 pounds and didn't sleep for 14 days straight. This terror lasted only about six months. He then began to heal on his own and in about a year he was completely over the issue. At this point he met with me for understanding and I noticed that he became free of his issues so quickly. He met a darling, new wife and has no jealousy issues with her whatsoever. He is not predisposed to rejection because it did not occur for him in his childhood.

In my opinion, when a trauma occurs later in life, cognitive (conscious) behavioral therapies are useful, such as affirmations, actions, choice, future focus, saying "no," etc., and childhood work is not as necessary.

(If you find that you get emotionally stuck during any part of this book, I suggest calling a therapist or coach to guide you through it. Or you may visit my web site, www.whatstopsyou.com, click on "Hints," for a list of NLP Master Practitioners in your area.) Most of the time, following the book format will be all you need to heal and move forward.)

Keep in mind: Studies show that the only real change that occurs is at an unconscious level.

Later stages of life manifest natural changes and transitions in the human life cycle. Whether the person had support and assistance or was denied stability and guidance as a child will predispose the individual, in adulthood, to swing to either side of the pendulum. For example, referring back to Erikson's model, from ages 20–30, a person will develop intimacy or become isolated. From ages 30–50, he or she may develop great generosity or become more stagnated in attitude and development. At age 55 and beyond, he or she develops integrity or leans more towards despair.

If you wish to learn more about Erikson's stages, consult any of his books. You may also reference these other books: *Transformations: Growth and Change in Adult Life* by Roger L. Gould, *Passages: Predictable Crises of Adult Life* by Gail Sheehy, and *The Seasons of a Man's Life* by Daniel J. Levinson.

If it is so important not to interrupt a child's development stages, then do we get to blame our parents for all our problems? Parents seem to constantly disrupt kids' stages of learning – for example, by simply insisting that their teens should come to the family Christmas party. If you refer to my list of stages, you will see that the child could associate the meaning that he or she is powerless and that he or she is giving up his or her identity by going to the party. The teen could make meaning/stories/fables that the family loves and accepts him or her because they are insisting that the teen go to the Christmas party. Children can make meanings in many ways based on many variables. How about a parent who scolds an eight-year-old for coming home after dark? Now the child may feel shamed. He may feel that he is not accountable, and his identity is crushed. Or, he may feel secure to know that his parents are concerned about him.

Well, what is a parent to do? It just seems really obvious that parents cause all of their kids' problems. Since parents have no manual for raising kids and most parents are making it up as they go, it is safe to say that parents don't do many things in the correct manner. You might say, "Wow, no wonder I have had such a hard time." Yet, here is the best example I can think of that explains why parents are off the hook.

The Tommy and Johnny Story

Once upon a time, a "perfect father" existed. He had two boys. He went downstairs to Tommy's room and said, "Tommy, you usually have a clean room, but right now it is quite messy. Company is coming over soon, so I need you to clean it up." Tommy said to himself, "Dad thinks I am usually clean. Wow, I am great." Next, the perfect dad went to Johnny's room and said, "Johnny, you usually have a clean room, but right now it is quite messy. Company is coming over soon, so I need you to clean it up." Johnny thought to himself, "Boy, Dad hates me. I can never do anything right. I give up!"

Both boys have made different meanings to the same request from their father.

Conflicts split the children. *You're a nerd! No, I'm not; so are you.*

I believe that all people are born good and innocent. As we age, we observe the world with a limited amount of information, and we begin to make meaning about what we do and about all that goes on around us. Our soul's predispositions and physical chemistry have a lot to do with how we make meaning. We make different meanings because of variables, such as right or left-brain cycles, biorhythms, family rules and roles, and many other explainable and unexplainable reasons. This chapter, however, will not necessarily focus on all the whys that we make different meanings; let us just settle for the fact that we all make meanings for assorted reasons. Fair enough?

Anna was enamored by all she was learning and by the concepts of stagnating stages of development. She had become aware of many things and had made positive changes in her life. She mentioned how so many of her old fables and stories had changed drastically, and she was writing positive stories about herself and others. She relayed how she was putting her new ways of thinking into actions as she increased her mental process and skill level. She said that she stood up tall and told her boyfriend to take a hike. She said her boyfriend was so shocked when she finally spewed it out that he looked as though he was embalmed in the standing position. She said it was plainly miraculous to finally feel that she was reconnecting to her own reality.

As the days melted into weeks, she began to radiate more of an abundance of vitality and energy. I told her that I still wanted to be very thorough with her and find any other issues of sabotage. She asked me how we could find out if she had any unhealed inner children. I told her there were four distinct ways to find them.

I recommend to my reader that you first just read the next section completely and then go back and work through your own issues. It is systematic with steps to discover and heal. After you have read Anna's example, you will be able to come back to this place and work through the steps with your own particular issues.

There are **four distinct ways** to find a time in your life that caused you to stagnate and leave an **inner child** behind:

1. The first way is to simply **remember a childhood memory** that has haunted your mind throughout your life – a time that you know has caused you to shift back to a less than desirable state of mind. OR...
2. Imagine being in a hot air balloon floating high above your life. See your birth through to the

current moment in an imaginary line that is about 6 to 10 feet long, down on the floor. Where are the metaphorical dark spots on your life? **Where did your limiting beliefs begin?** When did you begin to feel "stuck"? (This method is really easy to use.) OR...

3. Another way to find a stagnated time in your life is to acknowledge a constant, uncomfortable body feeling like a sinking heart, a closed throat, a pit in the stomach, or another bothersome body feeling. When you feel this common uncomfortable feeling, sit back, relax,  and acknowledge that the body part is communicating with the unconscious. Then just ask yourself, "How old does this part feel?" Is it a little baby, a grade-school kid, or a teenager acting out?

Sometimes it is difficult to understand that this part may have an age. By understanding that it does have a younger age, you can then be open to possibilities. Being more open allows this part to let you know its age. I know this may seem weird. Remember, weird is that which we do not understand. When you discover the age of this body part (stomach, throat, heart, etc.), you will begin to give this part some attention and stop fighting yourself so much. When you have an emotional stomachache, does it seem that your stomach is fighting you? Yes. So again, when you give attention to this part, it will stop fighting so hard. For now, just find the age of this part as you become aware. OR…

4. The fourth way is to feel the last time you experienced the uncomfortable body sensation. Turn up the uncomfortable physical feeling, allow your mind to relax, and allow the body part to glide you back in time. It may be just a week ago or as far back as your childhood. You will be surprised at how quickly the feeling will take you back. Acknowledge where it takes you. Relax, breathe, and ask it to take you back even further to its origin, and it may be so young that it might surprise you.

Hint:

Most imprints are coded in the throat, heart, or stomach. Uncommonly they appear as a headache, shoulder tension, or another sensation. Usually in my experience, if the client senses that it is other than the center of the body, the client is not aware that the start of the shoulder pain or headache is actually in the throat, heart, or stomach. However, there are always exceptions.

Anna said, "How interesting. As you were explaining the body parts communicating with the unconscious, I was feeling the deep, hollow feeling in my stomach that I felt in the first session. I was listening to your explanations and sure enough, it took me back in time. I have felt it constantly in my adult life. It took me back to high school when I felt vulnerable to others' thoughts or when I felt all alone."

She then gasped, "I remember! I remember when I first felt this feeling!" Her eyes were wide, as though she were a deer hypnotized by a car's headlights.

"Where?" I asked. "How old are you and what is going on?" (Notice that Anna was associated, while she told me about the situation.)

She said, "I am three years old, and I am swinging on a swing in the park by my house. I am so cute, and I have long, dark, silky braids. I am kinda mean to my little friend, and I pull her hair once in a while to tease her. I am swinging, singing to myself, and enjoying the air against my face. Then all of a sudden, someone comes up behind me and grabs one of my braids. They grab so hard that it stops me from swinging, and it hurts so badly that I think my braid is going to come out of my head. I turn around and in horror see my little friend's mother clutching my braid while holding open scissors against my hair.

"The mother said, 'If you ever pull my little girl's hair again, I am going to cut your pretty little braids off!'

"Then the mean lady just walked away with her scissors and a smug look on her face. I just sat there in emotional shock in my lifeless swing. I sat there a long time until no one was around and everyone had gone home. I don't remember how I got back to my house."

Anna looked at me as a drowning child would look at an adult, pleading for a rescue from a deep pool of murky water.

I told her to let her mind come back to the room, back to me. I comforted her and let her know that she was on the right path and that I was here beside her. I asked her to follow along on the next steps.

The Process of Healing

Daddy, make the bad man go away.

Step 1. Trace.

Now that you have found your imprint experience, it is necessary to stay there, be associated for about 1 to 30 seconds, feel the feelings, and experience what is going on. Acknowledge that the memory is painful.

Step 2. Step back.

Now remember the last chapter, in which I defined and explained dissociation? Well, now is the time to dissociate.

"Anna," I said, "come back to me here in the present. Go ahead, it's OK. Then stand up and shake that feeling off. Now sit in the other chair over there."

She was dumbfounded to realize that an experience from so long ago affected her today.

Hint:
Feelings that are buried alive
grow, breed, and have babies.

Step 3. Dissociate.

Dissociate from the scenario and notice positive beliefs before the experience.

I asked Anna to rewind the movie in her mind to about **one hour before the episode began.** Look at the cute little girl before the experience. What beliefs/stories is she making, in her mind, that are good?

Anna said:

- I was cute.
- I was likable.
- I was lovable.
- I was capable.
- Others were safe and helpful.
- The world was fun.

Step 4. Make a list of the limiting beliefs that just started at that exact moment.

"Now as you go forward in the movie, when the lady comes up behind you, at that exact moment, **what limiting beliefs did you develop in place of the positive beliefs that you had previously?"** I asked.

Slowly, she said that she believed:

- I am alone because my mom didn't come to my rescue.
- I am not safe.
- Cute is bad.
- I am not capable of defending myself.
- Others can hurt me.
- Others are not to be trusted.
- Others control me.
- The world is not to be trusted and is definitely scary!

"Good job discovering, Anna. You have become very aware of your body and emotions. Excellent! I know it is painful, and from this point on, most of the pain is over. We are now ready to change history.

"Yes, it is interesting that something that happened so long ago has had such an effect on you – something that is no longer real and something that is gone. You now understand the reality of muscle and cell memory, don't you? This event was coded in your body, and this is why all the talk therapy you have done was not complete."

Anna went on to explain how it all made conscious sense now. All her life since this event occurred, she had been afraid to be alone. She hadn't felt supported even when consciously, she ought to be OK. She commonly felt bad if she looked too good because looking good was bad, so she would sabotage herself to look worse than she did. She had trust issues with authority figures. She noticed that all areas of her life were affected by this monumental event.

"Wow!" Anna coughed.

Step 5. Visit your younger you (your inner child). Create a list of resources your younger self will need to go through this experience without a hitch.

This step will be an interesting and rewarding experience. Now that you logically understand what happened, I am going to ask you to see your younger self before the event, when she was OK. First, create a **list of resources** – resources that, **if** your younger self had them at the time of the event, would have helped you to be OK. Examples of resources are **faith, hope, wisdom, understanding, love, trust, forgiveness, perception, or others.** If she magically had some of these resources, she would be OK to realize that her friend's mom had issues and was just a woman who was reacting to her own emotions. She would also realize that her little self is really safe because she understands the perception of her friend's mom. Better still, what if her little self had known the lady was coming up behind her, so she was prepared and could have run or turned around and said, "Oh no, you don't"? There are many ways she could have made the scenario turn out differently, right?

As we created the list, Anna began to feel hopeful. She became enamored in the process and sat up in her chair as though we were really going to go back in time to help.

We came up with the following resources to give to her younger self:

- A warning that the mom was coming
- Faith
- Boundaries
- Feeling supported and not alone
- Understanding
- Perspective
- Love
- Forgiveness

Step 6: Your future self visits you.

"Anna, imagine there is a knock on the door. In walks a stunning woman about 70 years old. We wonder who in the world is intruding on our session. She comes in and pulls up a chair and looks directly into your eyes. She says slowly, **'Hi. I am you, Anna, from the future.** I am here to help you. I have been where you are, in Darlene's office. I remember being where you are. I remember feeling what you feel. I have lived your whole life with you, and I am sorry I have not let you know that I was there for you. I am here now with you. I will always be with you, always. I know your every thought and action. I want you to know that I have progressed past this issue that you are currently experiencing, and I am successful in business and in relationships.'

"Future Anna continues to tell you about what lies ahead in your future – specifically about your grandchildren, where you live, and what business success you have experienced.

"The future Anna says, 'Anna, I will always be with you, and I will see you in some years.' She gives you some advice and then walks out the door.

"Now, if that really happened, can you imagine what it would do for you? You would instantly have faith in the future. You would feel supported and connected. You would feel secure and hopeful, wouldn't you? You would know many things about your future, and most specifically that you didn't die today, because none of us know that we won't die today, right? You would know you lived through this time in your life and would benefit from this visit that had given you so much."

This experience enveloped Anna in deep reflection. We sat in silence for quite a while.

Step 7: Remember the positive feeling and hold it in your body.

Resources need to be **in your body** before you give them away to your younger self. I asked Anna to think of one of these resources – for example, to think of a time that she had self-love – a time she really loved herself. She remembered a brief time when she had a party and a popular girl came. She felt really important, capable, and full of self-confidence. I asked her **to turn up the feeling and hold it in her body.** Now give that feeling to your younger self. The stronger the feeling is in your body, the better, and the more you are experiencing it full-body.

Step 8: Give the listed resources to your younger self.

In your mind's eye, I want you to go over to your younger self one hour before the event. Get in rapport with her before you tell her who you are. Ask her questions about herself and match her body language. Then tell her who you are. Now project this self-love that you have **in your body,** to her, in any creative way that works for you. Notice how she receives it. Notice how she responds differently now.

Now tell her that you are from the future and you have some cool things to give her. Tell her that in about an hour, her friend's mom is going to come over to her while she is swinging. Tell her what will happen and what won't happen. **Tell her the situation is OK and you will be with her.** Tell her that her friend's mom has her own problems and that this little act will be a way for this mom to try to feel better. Tell her that you will be back in a second because you have to go back and consult with your coach to know the next step. Ask her if she is OK for now. Look at her. Is she OK? Stay with her until she is fine with you leaving for a moment.

What does she need next? Give her perspective. Teach her how to float out of her body (dissociate) and look at herself. Teach her to float into her friend (other) when she pulled her hair. Have her notice how it felt (empathy) to have little Anna pull her hair. **Have some fun with her, floating in and out of people.** Show her how to imagine she is Anna's dog getting excited to go to the park. When she is ready, have her imagine that she is the friend's mom with scissors coming up to that little girl on the swing. Hmm, you feel pretty mad, don't you? Kind of out of control yet protective of your little girl?

Have her **return** to her little self and tell her that you will be back after you consult with your coach again.

So how is she looking? Better? What else does she need?

Anna decided to give her younger, inner child a **Bugs Bunny attitude: "Hey, what's up, Ma?"** Her friend's mom looked surprised that little Anna wasn't scared. She then gave her younger self the observer perspective of realizing this is just one moment in time. She did this by taking her younger self into the sky, way above the issue, and seeing herself down there among all the other people in the world having issues. She imagined her future and saw that this was not the last issue she would have in her life.

Then Anna gave her inner child a huge hug and let her know that she was not alone. She would always be with her. She gave her a pretty, pretend brush and comb and said it was OK to be so cute.

Little three-year-old Anna was turning into a bionic child, full of wonderful adult resources, full of all the resources to get her through this time safely and without a hitch. I asked Anna to nurture her younger self in any way that was appropriate. She gave her younger self a final hug and, with tears in her eyes, imagined she was her younger self being nurtured by her older self.

Does little Anna need anything else before we allow her to grow up to her current age? "No, she is great, just great," Anna said.

Step 9: Associate into your younger self and feel all the great resources as though you had been born with them. Grow up through every moment in time.

Go ahead and stay in your younger self; feel all the resources you have been given. As you breathe, hold all the resources in your body, and imagine growing older with all these resources inside you. Notice growing older in a new way, through every moment in time, each year becoming better and better. All the resources grow with you, and you notice how negative experiences are different, aren't they? Grow through each day and night, older and older, until you reach your current age, taking all the time you need in this next moment. Let me know when you are at your current age, and then we'll move on to the next step.

Step 10: Future pace.

Now as you are here with me in this new perspective, you notice what is different and what is working.

Now look into **the future.** What have you always dreamed about? What has your mind done in the privacy of your secret-day-dreams? What have you dreamt you would be, and what you would do? Let that dream grow into reality as you begin **to see yourself** in the future, in the next week at a time when these resources will come in handy. See yourself in the **future** and notice what you do, what you focus on, and what life is like with these resources.

Step 11: Come back to the present moment.

"Hi, welcome back. Now please get a drink of water," I said. "If you'd like, go ahead and take a walk around my mountain park located across the street. Walk until you feel less disoriented. Movement and water will help all the learning to soak in."

To my reader: If it is appropriate for you – if you have discovered a part of you that seems to be an inner child who needs assistance – then go ahead and move through the 11 steps as Anna did. Be thorough with each step. I repeat the steps and guide you through them in a moment. **If you feel "stuck," simply stand up, step back, and remember that this is all pretend anyway.** Your inner child is only a memory, so you can lighten up about it. If you are still stuck, remember that you have been stuck for so many years that you can live a little longer with this issue. Right? Maybe you will want to revisit the issue at a later time when you are more ready. Maybe you are ready now. Either way, you will learn something because life is a journey.

Now, it is your turn. If it helps to keep you focused, have someone you trust, read you the questions and guide you through the steps.

STEP 1: TRACE.

Please refer to the preceding pages for the four ways to find your inner child. Choose the technique that is best for you.

What is your experience?

_____
_____
_____
_____

STEP 2: STEP BACK, dissociate, shake off the feeling, and sit in another chair.

What is your experience?

_____
_____
_____
_____

STEP 3: DISSOCIATE completely and see your inner you over there. (Now notice your positive beliefs before the experience.)

What are his/her (your inner you) positive beliefs before the experience when they were OK?

_____
_____

_____

_____

STEP 4: MAKE A LIST OF THE LIMITING BELIEFS that started at THAT EXACT MOMENT (beliefs about yourself, others, and the world in general).

What are the new limiting beliefs?

_____

_____

_____

_____

STEP 5: VISIT YOUR YOUNGER YOU (your inner child).

Go over to your younger you. Say "Hi," get in rapport first, and then tell your younger self who you are: your future self. Notice your younger self's reaction. Tell your younger self that you have some cool stuff to give him or her from the future. Say that you will be back in a moment.

Create a list of resources your younger self will need to go through this experience without a hitch.

What resources does your inner you need to be OK in this experience (hope, love, wisdom, understanding, acceptance, self-love, etc.)?

_____

_____

_____
_____

STEP 6: YOUR FUTURE SELF VISITS YOU. If the you-of-the-future came to visit, what would it be like?

What is your experience?

_____
_____
_____
_____

STEP 7: REMEMBER THE POSITIVE FEELING. Get the positive resource by remembering a time you had it, and then hold that feeling in your body.

When did you have one of the resources that you listed? It may just be a simple time – a time you had that resource fully and completely.

_____
_____
_____
_____

STEP 8: GIVE THE LISTED RESOURCES TO YOUR YOUNGER SELF.

Now get the next resource in your body and give it to your younger self. Then get the next resource and continue until your younger self has all the resources you listed.

What is your experience?

_____
_____
_____
_____

STEP 9: ASSOCIATE INTO YOUR YOUNGER SELF and grow up to your current age.

Feel all the great resources as though you had been born with them. Grow through every moment in time, imagining every day and every night and noticing how things would have been different had you known these resources. Things would have been different, wouldn't they?

What is your experience?

_____
_____
_____
_____

STEP 10: FUTURE PACE.

Picture yourself in the future with **all** these wonderful resources. When, in the next week, will these resources come in handy? See yourself with all the resources. What are you like in the future with all the resources?

What is your experience?

_____
_____
_____
_____

STEP 11: COME BACK TO THE PRESENT MOMENT.

What is your experience?

_____

_____

_____

_____

How did you do? Please get a drink of water and walk around a bit. After completing an exercise such as this, the unconscious needs time to integrate or soak in the new way of thinking and acting. Give yourself a few days to let it all settle in. Recognize that there may be other injured children **within,** and you can address them later. Be nice to yourself, and remember, you are special!

Evidence of Change

At our next session, I asked Anna where her three-year-old self was. She paused for quite a while, looked around, and finally said, "Here, in my heart. She is not anywhere really; she is me."

That was the right answer, because think about it: If the inner child is healed, it would grow up, right? The inner child would not be separate from you; he or she would have evolved into you.

Anna reported more self-esteem, more confidence, and more trust for life. The best part is that she didn't feel the hole in her stomach at all that week, which was new and different because the hole had been her constant, nagging companion until now. She was so grateful.

My reward comes when I see a smile on a face that before only had frown lines etched in the skin.

What do I want to be when I grow up?

When we venture into healing, we acknowledge and heal the past, honor the **present,** and create the future. Let's talk about the **present.** There are two profound books that I have read about the **present.** The first is *The Precious Present* by Spencer Johnson, and the second is *The Power of Now: A Guide to Spiritual Enlightenment* by Eckhart Tolle.

The first book, *The Precious Present*, is about a young boy who meets an old man who seems to be perfectly happy. The boy wants to model the old man and asks him how he achieved this happiness. The old man says that it is a precious present that the boy must discover for himself. In this small and profound book, the young boy searches the world over for the precious present. As the years pass, he becomes  weary in his useless search. He returns home empty-handed and finds the old man, who is now on his deathbed. The young man becomes angry and bitter about not being able to find the precious present. The old man tells the young man to go to the hills and sit quietly. He explains that the young man already has the present. He had it all the while and just needed to realize it. The young man takes his advice and, as he sits quietly by a large, intriguing tree, suddenly his old ways of thinking shatter instantly!

His epiphany has arrived. He understands that the precious present is just that: **the present moment.** Yes, he had it all the time; each and every moment is the present. Now he begins to sink into despair, knowing he has wasted each moment of the present searching the world in vain. He quickly snaps out of it, realizing that he does not want to give up this profound present moment. He goes forward teaching others about the precious present.

One of the best ways I've found to become present is to simply imagine the past on one side of you and your future on the other. Acknowledge both and then take your hand and cast a shadow over your desk or lap. Realize that the shadow is in the present moment, and know that joy is felt only in the present moment. Joy does not exist in the past or the future. Begin to see and feel the shadow and become present. Feel joy because the only thing that exists in the whole world is now, right now. Take pleasure in the joy.

What are the results of being present? Well, let me ask you this question. Think of a person or persons you enjoy being with more than anyone else; someone whose company you enjoy and whom you really like. Now is it right that the reason you like them and enjoy them so much is because they accept you just as you are? I imagine that the answer is "yes." Now is it also true that this person is present with you and not living in the distant past or in the far future? He or she is right with you, presently looking, listening, and being attentive. I imagine your answer is also "yes." The greatest gifts you can give to others are to accept them just as they are and to be present with them.

"Of course," Anna said. "I see why I am more attractive to others these days – in addition to the fact that I am markedly thinner. I understand why I am more present with others, because I am getting out of my stuff and am able to focus on the present. I must have been a project that people would see coming. I have often imagined that as I entered a room, the people would suddenly exit as I came in dragging my past emotions and experiences riddled all over the outside of me. Such a simple thing, and it took all these years to find some answers. Although right now I can feel myself slipping into regret just like your story of the young boy, feeling like I had wasted my life. OK, enough of that regret. I'm shaking it off and staying in the present moment with you, Darlene. Thanks for the info."

Joy can only be felt in the present moment.

We have sorted the past and acknowledged the present, and now we will open a space for the future. When you came in for your first session, Anna, you commented that your future was black. This is very common for depressed individuals. I would maintain that nearly 100 percent of all depressed individuals see only black in the future. In fact, if you want to feel bad some day, just white out your future; it works every time. (Depression also focuses on what you don't have and what you won't have in the future instead of what you do have now.)

Purpose/Mission

We have now opened a beautiful place for your future. At this point we can gaze forward towards your purpose and mission. What is your purpose? Why are you alive? What will you do tomorrow and why? What do you want indelibly etched on your gravestone when you complete your mission here in this frail existence?

When contemplating our purpose and mission, we think about the future and our sense of more than ourselves. We realize that our purpose relates to our sense of who we are. Knowing who we are affects our mission and actions that support our higher reasons for living. Spiritual-level experiences have to do with our sense of being part of something more than ourselves on a very deep and connected level. Neurologically, our purpose is manifested in our aura or countenance.

Since our future is not real, we can dream and create what we would like to be and do in the years to come. Please complete the following enlightening exercise to help form and fashion your future self.

The Pyramid of Thought

Opening the Future, Ramble-Writing Exercise:

Write a paragraph or a few pages to describe what you want in the future in the following five categories.

After you have ramble-written and feel that you are done writing, then switch to your nondominant hand and write some more. You will be surprised at how you are able to continue to feel and express a few words or sentences with your nondominant hand.

What do you want? Physically:

_____

_____

_____

_____

What do you want? Socially:

_____

_____

_____

_____

What do you want? Emotionally:

_____

_____

_____

_____

What do you want? Intellectually:

_____

_____

_____

_____

What do you want? Spiritually:

_____

_____

_____

_____

Please summarize each paragraph into one sentence:

Physical: _____

Social: _____

Emotional: _____

Intellectual: _____

Spiritual: _____

Now **summarize each sentence into one word** for each category so you will have five words.

Write the five words below.

1. _____
2. _____
3. _____
4. _____
5. _____

Please summarize these five words into one word.

Word: _____

Now summarize this one word into a symbol. What is your symbol?

Symbol: _____

May you remember this symbol, always!

Now that you have a sense of your future, let's complete your future vision. After we create this vision with detail, I will ask you to step into it, **associated,** and feel the excitement of time travel into the future.

Future Vision

What I would like you to do is imagine seeing your whole physical body in front of you in about one week's time. What do you look like physically? You have a great imagination, so make it good.

Now see yourself physically one year from now, the way you want to be. Make yourself just the way you want to be in a year, inside and out. See yourself from the front, sides, and back. Lift, scoop, scrape, and color yourself. See yourself on the inside as well. What do the insides of your lungs look like? Continue until you look great. Breathe.

See yourself now, socially, just the way you want yourself to be in one year's time. How do you act? What are you doing? How do you feel and respond?

See yourself now, emotionally, the way you want yourself to be in about a year. Change the picture until you are just right. See your mannerisms and countenance. Breathe.

Now see yourself intellectually. What do you focus on? What are you studying or learning?

In addition to all of the above, see yourself now the way you want yourself to be spiritually. Notice the light you radiate. Notice your symmetrical movements.

Now notice your relationships and envision just how you want them to be in one year. Keep in mind you can only change yourself and not others, so focus on yourself, how you respond and move, what you choose to focus on, and how you behave.

What will you be like financially? See it the way you want in detail, down to the very penny.

Now see your career in one year. Go for it; shoot for the moon.

Look at yourself in one year's time, in terms of self-care. How does your future self care for you in terms of boundaries and self-love and honor?

And now, see your Purpose and Mission. See yourself, out there, one year in the future. See how you are a part of the whole world, not separate from it. See how you behave and interact through service and acknowledgment of others. Create this picture in a powerful way as you take in a huge breath and then slowly breathe out.

If you would, review your future self. Realize that as you created this picture, you did not create your world around yourself, nor did you attempt to change others – did you? This picture of yourself ought to remain the same whether you live in Africa in a year, whether you are married or not, or whether you are in Florida or Nebraska. You are you, no matter where you are.

Take a look and see if there is anything else you want to add or shift.

Now gently step into your future self as you breathe yourself in. Take a long moment. What does it feel like to have this body you have now and racing metabolism?

When Anna completed this exercise, she breathed, she smiled, she gleamed, and she emanated light.

"Anna," I said, "Please, now, turn around and see your present self in my office. Can you see your present self on the couch? As you see her, you do remember being her, don't you? You remember all the stuff you were going through. You remember wondering if great changes would stick and what life would be like if you were thin and in control. You are now one year older. As you see yourself one year older, and full of new resources, what advice would you give yourself?"

What I would like you, the reader, to do now is to turn back around and gaze into **your** future. Look ahead three years. What will you be like in all 10 life categories? How about in five years? You just keep getting better, don't you? Now in 10 years? How about 15? How about 20? What about 30? What about age 60, 70, 80, 90, 120 years old, 200 years old? How about 300 years old? Breathe. As you continue, your soul gets more refined as you progress towards 500 years old and on through eternity, doesn't it?

Please write the **advice you would give yourself if you magically became one year older** with all of the new resources you need alive in you.

Here is the advice that I would give myself, if I were one year older and could see myself, one year in past.

_____

_____

_____

_____

Chapter Fifteen:

EVALUATING YOUR PERFORMANCE

Where Are You Now?

66 "**A**nna," I said, "For your final weekly session, before we begin meeting monthly, I would like you to fill out the Balanced Living Wheel again."

After she filled out the wheel again, she exclaimed, "Wow!" as she plopped back on the couch. "I am a completely different person."

I said, **"No, you are the same person,** with new ways of thinking and now your positive qualities can shine through. You have learned actions, skills, and mental processes and have implemented these learnings. Now it is time to maintain where you are today."

Balanced Living Wheel
Self-Assessment

Name: *Anna*
My Professional Goal: <u>Make comfortable sales calls</u>
My Personal Goal: <u>Lose 25 pounds</u>

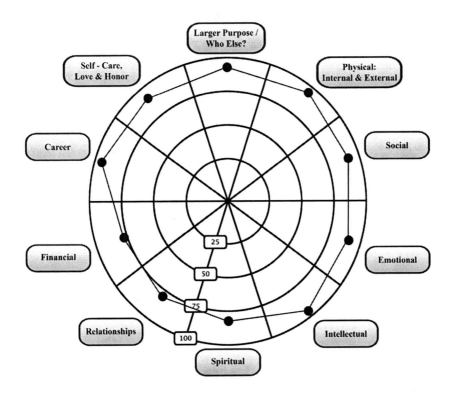

Anna's Assessment *after her journey*

Anna's journey began last fall, and now on this new spring morning, Anna is excited and proud of her progress.

Now it is time for you, my reader, to retake your Balanced Living Wheel Self-Assessment. Compare your results with your original assessment and focus on what you have done well. I recommend that you retake the test monthly or quarterly. Since life has it's ups and downs you will want to monitor where you are, often, so that you can navigate through life in a powerful way, full of choice.

Remember you can upload a free copy of the Wheel by going to www.whatstopsyou.com For more information see the Appendix.

Have fun sharing the Wheel with your friends, parents, kids, and co-workers.

Balanced Living Wheel
Self-Assessment

Name: _____ Date:_____
My Professional Goal: _____
My Personal Goal: _____

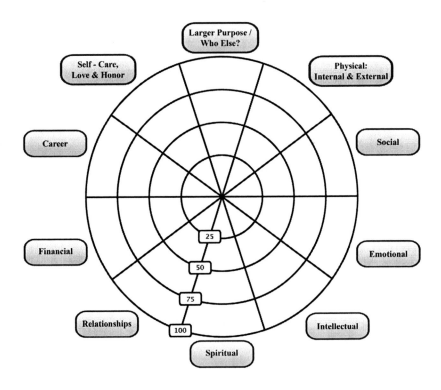

Your Assessment *after your journey*

© 2006 Darlene Braden, db & company.
Permission is granted to copy this page with instructions, provided **no** modifications are made. To purchase the book *What Stops You?*, go to www.whatstopsyou.com.

Just as one would go on maintenance for weight control after they had reached their ideal weight, you need to have a plan to maintain your balanced living and making your life work.

1. Have you set a daily, a monthly, and a yearly plan for yourself? What are they?

_____

_____

_____

_____

2. Do you know how to assess where you are, and what you need to do, to take action? How and what?

_____

_____

_____

_____

"Are you excited for your future?" I asked. "Absolutely!" Anna said.

Please answer both personally and professionally:

What actions will you take?

_____

_____

_____

_____

What skills have you developed?

_____

_____

_____

_____

What mental processes have you discovered and shifted?

_____

_____

_____

_____

What are your new DREAMS?

_____

_____

_____

_____

Anna's sessions are now on a monthly basis. As she comes into my office on this bright and sunny morning in early spring, I look at her twice and see a young girl waltzing through my door. Light shines from her eyes. She is living in the present moment, not living in her past. Her hair is as healthy as it was in high school, and her walk is chipper. As she sits down, I see an actualized individual full of love, intensity, and purpose. She looks so beautiful. I see a tiny little body, firm and fit, frosting her radiant spirit. She says aloud that **she loves life.** She is **in** that cute body of hers instead of avoiding her feelings.

We start talking right away about how we love each other's sexy sandals and where we were going for vacations this summer. As the conversation continues, I learn that she is in an amazing relationship with a real, honest guy with integrity – a good man. The great thing is that she knows she deserves it. No doubt! Her business is thriving, and making calls is fun and enlightening for her. She has coached many others about the actions, skills, and mental processes of sales, and she also enjoys offering free services to one client a month. Her trust and love for strangers have increased, and she has found true meaning and contentment in life.

She gleams when she tells her exciting news of reconnecting with her precious children. They finally respect Anna, and she is able to share what she has learned while they make plans for the future as a family. Her daughter is expecting her first child. Talking about possible names and darling clothing cheers up Anna's day. Her son is strong and supportive. He loves and cares for his mother, and they have a newfound, fulfilling relationship.

Anna keeps her *What Stops You?* book and the notebook that she has been using close at hand, and as she skips through this life, she realizes the need for maintenance and constant openness. She has shared her learnings with friends and has become a valuable listening ear for many people. She realizes that life is a journey.

We will proceed to meet monthly as she continues to learn more about self-esteem, connection, and trust. What a great woman. I am honored to be in her life.

Acknowledging God and his plans for us assists us in looking at life from a larger perspective. What is your mission in this life? How is your life part of a greater purpose that reaches far beyond you? How will the "I Am" statements about yourself grow and develop as you pull them into your body and let them emanate from your skin, through the air to the whole world and beyond? Let go of thought and reason; trust in the **Almighty Being** that already knows what and who you are. Walk through life as though you are weightless and attuned to the drift of God's wind. With clear diction, ask sincerely, "Dear Lord, what would you have me do today?"

I thank you from my soul for sharing yourself with me at this time in your life. I am better because you live. Thank you for being you, and know deeply that I support you in your journey.

Sincerely with love,

Darlene

We appreciate referrals:

As you reflect upon your progress during the course of this book, please take this opportunity to share your experience with people you care about. Who do you know that might possibly benefit from learning about internal conflicts, limiting beliefs and how to find peace in their lives? Tell them about this book and how to order it.

For the benefit of others, please take the time to post what you have learned on the **What Stops You?** Website at www.whatstopsyou.com. What helped the most? What did you learn that was most profound? Your testimonial and advice will be greatly appreciated.

About the author

Darlene Braden brings to her clients a breadth of knowledge and practical experience. She draws from a wide variety of personal empowerment tools ranging all the way from Eastern philosophy to modern, tangible techniques. She helps her clients to address issues on a behavioral level with external challenges or on a deeper level concerning unconscious awareness.

Darlene holds a B.S. in Human Development and Family Studies from the University of Utah. She has received certifications as a Clinical Hypnotherapist, Master Neuro Linguistic Programming (NLP) Practitioner, NLP Health Practitioner, and Reiki Master. She has completed the Alcohol and Drug Abuse Treatment Training Program at the University of Utah and has worked in secure delinquent facilities. She has had success as a professional platform speaker, corporate trainer, and business/life coach.

With boundless energy and a true joy for life, she has also become a top aerobics instructor, avid runner, and fitness professional while raising five successful children. She is also a composer and singer and has published two songs.

She currently has a behavioral consulting practice, in Sandy, Utah.

Appendix:

ADDITIONAL RESOURCES

The Balanced Living Wheel Self-Assessment

**Download your FREE copy of
the Balanced Living Wheel Self-Assessment today,
with instructions!**

To download your **free** copy of The Balanced Living Wheel Self-Assessment with instructions, go to www.whatstopsyou.com. Permission is granted to copy the Wheel for your own personal and professional use as long as **no** modifications are made to the Wheel and the instructions. In addition, **each page must include the *What Stops You?* website address.**

If you find that you get emotionally stuck during any part of this book, I suggest that you ask a therapist or coach to guide you through it. Or you may visit my web site. www.whatstopsyou.com, and click on "Hints" for a list of NLP Master Practitioners in your area.

Recommended Reading

Bateson, Gregory. *Steps to an Ecology of Mind: Collected Essays in Anthropology, Psychiatry, Evolution, and Epistemology.* Chicago: University of Chicago Press, 1972.

Dilts, Robert. *Changing Belief Systems with NLP.* Capitola, CA: Meta Publications, 1990.

Erikson, Erik H. *Identity and the Life Cycle.* New York: W. W. Norton & Company, Inc., 1994.

Gould, Roger L., M.D. *Transformations: Growth and Change in Adult Life.* New York: Simon & Schuster, 1979.

Hellinger, Bert. *Love's Hidden Symmetry: What Makes Love Work in Relationships.* Redding, CT: Zeig, Tucker & Theisen, Inc., 1998.

Johnson, Spencer. *The Precious Present.* New York: Doubleday, 1984.

Levinson, Daniel J. *The Seasons of a Man's Life.* New York: Ballantine Books, 1978.

Sheehy, Gail. *Passages: Predictable Crises of Adult Life.* New York: E. P. Dutton & Co., 1976.

Tolle, Eckhart. *The Power of Now: A Guide to Spiritual Enlightenment.* Novato, CA: New World Library, 1999.

286938